THE BEST
AFTER-DINNER
SPORTS TALES

THE BEST AFTER-DINNER SPORTS TALES

Compiled by
Will Chignell

CollinsWillow

An Imprint of HarperCollins*Publishers*

First published in Great Britain in 2002 by CollinsWillow,
an imprint of HarperCollins*Publishers* London

Copyright © Compilation 2002 Will Chignell

 3 5 7 9 8 6 4 2

A CIP catalogue record for this book
is available from the British Library

The HarperCollins website address
is: www.**fire**and**water**.com

ISBN 0-00-714819-4

Printed and bound in Great Britain by
Clays Ltd, St Ives Plc

Picture acknowledgements
ALLSPORT: 1(t), 3(t), 4(bl & br), 6(b), 8(t), 9(t), 10(t), 11(b), 13(b), 14, 15, 16.
COLORSPORT: 1(b), 3(b), 6(tr), 7(t), 12(t), 13(t).
EMPICS: 2(t), 4(t), 5, 6(tl), 7(b), 8(b), 10(b), 11(t), 12(b).
PATRICK EAGAR: 9(b).
CARL FOGARTY'S PRIVATE COLLECTION: 2(b).

Health, happiness, laughter and sport – a heady concoction.

This book is dedicated to all children
who dream of just being healthy.

CONTENTS

E

Malcolm EDMUNDS
John EDRICH
Jonathan EDWARDS
Tracy EDWARDS
John EMBUREY
Farokh ENGINEER

F

Nick FALDO
Andrew FARRELL
John FEAVER
Carl FOGARTY
Duncan FORBES
Mark FOSTER
John FRANCOME

G

Kirsty GALLACHER
John GALLACHER
Jason GANNER
John R GARNER
Warren GATLAND
Calum GILES
Nick GILLINGHAM
Graham GOOCH
Graham GOODE
David GOWER
Herol GRAHAM
Tom GRAVENEY
Lucinda GREEN
Will GREEN
Will GREENWOOD
Danny GREWCOCK
Sally GUNNELL
Reg GUTTERIDGE

H

Keith HACKETT
Andrew HARRIMAN
Rod HARRINGTON
Miles HARRISON
Guy HARWOOD
Gavin HASTINGS
Scott HASTINGS
Rob HAWTHORNE
Alex HAY
Eddie HEMMINGS
Bill HIGGINSON
Alistair HIGNELL
Richard HILL
Richard HILL
Simon HODGKINSON
Carl HOGG
Damian HOPLEY
Tim HORAN
Mark HOWELL
Rob HOWLEY
Will HOY

I

John INVERDALE

J

Brian JACKS
Steve JAMES
Charles JEFFREY
Neil JENKINS
Paddy JOHNS
Ian JONES
Sally JONES

K

Chris KAMARA
Frank KEATING
Sean KERLY
Alex KING
Jack KYLE

L

Mark LAWRENSON
Graeme LE SAUX
Francis LEE
Donal LENIHAN
Jason LEONARD
Josh LEWSEY
Sean LINEEN
Gary LINEKER
Bill LLENGICH
David LLOYD
Kenny LOGAN
Jonah LOMU
Dan LUGER
Dan LYLE
Sandy LYLE
Michael LYNAGH
Cornelius LYSAGHT

M

Rod MacQUEEN
Rodney MARSH
Tommy MARTYN
Jason McATEER
John McCRIRICK
Glen McCRORY
Brian McDERMOTT
Alan McINALLY
Duncan McKENZIE
Bill McLAREN

Gordon McQUEEN

Stan MELLOR

Nigel MELVILLE

Katharine MERRY

Diane MODAHL

Dewi MORRIS

John MOTSON

Scott MURRAY

N

Phil NEAL

O

Martin OFFIAH

John OLVER

Conor O'SHEA

P

Eric PETERS

Agustin PICHOT

Lester PIGGOTT

Richard PITMAN

Pat POCOCK

Richard POOL-JONES

Budge POUNTNEY

David POWELL

Julie PULLIN

Q

Niall QUINN

Scott QUINNELL

R

Neal RADFORD

Ray REARDON

David REES

Dean RICHARDS

David RIPLEY

Ian ROBERTSON

John ROBERTSON

Mark ROBSON

Tim RODBER

Peter RODRIGUES

Dave ROGERS

Tony RUDLIN

S

Jamie SALMON

Dean SAMPSON

Hans SEGERS

Fergus SLATTERY

Alan SMITH

James M SMITH

Robin SMITH

Wayne SMITH

Steve SMITH-ECCLES

David SNELL

Gareth SOUTHGATE

David SPEEDIE

Mike STEPHENSON

Alec STEWART

Mattie STEWART

Stuart STOREY

Walter SWINBURN

T

Johnny TAPIA

Bob TAYLOR

Dennis TAYLOR

Graham TAYLOR

John TAYLOR

Mark TAYLOR

Peter TAYLOR

Dave THOMAS

Derek THOMPSON

Andrew THORNTON

Bill THRELFALL

Mike TINDALL

Daniel TOPOLSKI

Andy TOWNSEND

Gregor TOWNSEND

Tim TREMLETT

Meriel TUFNELL

Phil TUFNELL

Rob TURNER

U

Rory UNDERWOOD

V

Braam VAN STRAATEN

David VINE

W

Sid WADDELL

Rob WAINWRIGHT

Peter WALKER

Jim WATT

Jan WEBSTER

Peter WEST

Peter WHEELER

Chris WHITE

Julian WHITE

Steve WILD

Jonny WILKINSON

Bob WILSON

Sir Peter YARRANTON

Y

Phil YATES

Neil YOUNG

ACKNOWLEDGMENTS

—— • ◆ • ——

If you're like me, this is the part of a book that you normally just skip over, which is a shame because *The Best After-Dinner Sports Tales* simply could not have been produced without the help, advice, time and generosity of the people below. So if you've got a moment, please have a look; they certainly deserve your acknowledgment.

Thank you so much to all the contributors and cartoonists, Bill Beaumont, the SPARKS team – particularly Helen Farquharson – Tom Whiting and Michael Doggart of HarperCollins, Toby Hornett, Pete Dunlop, Neil Durden-Smith, all the producers at Sky for their time and patience, particularly Barney Francis, Martin Turner and Julian Maddock. A huge thank you to Sam Mclaughlan, James Stanley, George Chignell, Jon Holding, Simon Drakeford, Duncan Maclay, Mark Robson, Rupert Vitoria, Damian Hopley and the PRA, Adam Smith, Dickie Davis, Sarah Botham, Jill Douglas, Rod Studd, Di Endersby, Matt Coates, Jamie Monro, Hector Proud of Idea Generation, Jamie Jarvis of SFX, Daphne Short of Middlesex CCC, Tony Husband Cartoons – by permission of *The Times* – ERIC, the LTA, Lynne Collins of the British Cartoonists Club, Kate Blackwell of Lighthouse, Simon Laird of Craigie Taylor, Louise Patterson of the PGA European Tour and many others who have gone out of their way to help. Lastly, but most importantly, I would like to thank my wife Lu, who has been a true saint in putting up with my obsession to compile the book.

Will Chignell

FOREWORD

———— • ◆ • ————

In my day job, I put all my efforts into preventing goals. In contrast, my aim as SPARKS President 2002 is to score as big and often as possible in raising funds for children's medical research.

I am sure this book will be a great success. Never before has such an amusing and diverse group of tales been brought together in one collection, by such a glittering array of sporting celebrities. It will, no doubt, become the Bible for any aspiring after-dinner sports speaker! Furthermore, I'm delighted that all author royalties are being donated to SPARKS.

SPARKS aims to give all children a healthy start in life by funding vital medical research into the conditions that affect newborn babies and children. Raising money from corporate partnerships, major gifts and sporting and social events, SPARKS has contributed in excess of £8,000,000 over the past ten years. In 2001 alone, SPARKS raised £1,000,000; my goal is to help the charity top that figure in 2002.

Happy reading, and I hope you have as many laughs as I did!

Ray Clemence MBE
SPARKS President 2002

INTRODUCTION

I was delighted when approached by Will Chignell and SPARKS to write an introduction to his excellent book.

After-dinner speaking can give you a great thrill when things are going well, but it can be a lonely place standing up in front of 400 people and you are dying on your feet!

The first lesson of after-dinner speaking is to speak first; it is never wise to follow speakers who are better than you. If you are speaking last, make sure that you are on your feet before midnight. The drunker the audience, the harder it is for the speaker; in other words, they couldn't care less what you are saying. The only advantage is that they will have eaten the bread rolls!

As a speaker you always have to remember that the dinner you are attending is their biggest night of the year, so you have to be as enthusiastic as possible. You might be presenting the 'Clubman of the Year' award for the fifth night running, and you often find that the club's Master of Ceremonies is more interested in hearing his own voice than yours. In fact, most Master of Ceremonies are a pain in the backside and normally tell a few sad jokes, prolong the evening and bore the audience.

A good way of starting your own speech is, 'Having listened to the Master of Ceremonies for the last two hours, I cannot tell you how delighted I am to be on my feet ....'

Nowadays, most professional sportsmen receive advice on how to present themselves in front of an audience, whether it's the media or the general public, but during the dim and distant past this was not the case. Being an England rugby captain does not automatically make you a good after-dinner speaker! Many people assume that as a captain you can speak in public, but the standard speech for an England captain is at the post-match international dinner where all you do is thank the selectors and grovel to them in the hope you get reselected the following season.

I can remember one of my first speeches when I was invited to talk at Stourbridge Rugby Club in 1978. One of the guests was a New Zealand rugby player, Brad Johnson, who was touring at the time with the All Blacks, who were due to play England a month later at Twickenham. When the time for speeches arrived, I got to my feet having had little preparation and mumbled for about ten minutes on what England were going to do to the All Blacks. It was rubbish – and, as it turned out, so was our performance against them. I later returned to the Stourbridge Club where one of the members congratulated me on having improved at speech-making!

They say that a week is a long time in politics. Well, I can assure you that 30 to 40 minutes on your feet speaking when it is not being well received is a long time. If things are not going well, then the only thing to do is give the audience what you feel is your best story. In my case I always come out with the Erica Roe tale, which is later in the book. If that fails, then you really are in trouble.

I once gave a speech at a dinner which HRH Prince Edward was attending. Normally when you are speaking, the audience tends to be focused on you but in this case everybody was looking at him to gauge his reaction. Fortunately he seemed to be enjoying the speech, which was a massive relief to myself!

Sometimes one of the guests will come up to you when you

are sitting down to dinner and say that they heard you last week and hope that you have some new stories. As a sportsman you always have the opportunity to update your speech by talking about the sports topic of the day. When I was a team captain on the BBC's 'A Question of Sport', which is pre-recorded, it was always good fun to inform the audience of the likely winner of the forthcoming programme!

There is an expression: 'If it isn't broke then don't fix it', and I think this applies to public speaking. I always keep to my standard stories and if some of the audience have heard them before, then hard luck.

Some of the best sportsman speakers I have heard tend to be people who have spent a lot of time in dressing rooms, listening to players take the mickey out of each other. Among these, I think cricketers, in particular, are excellent. I could listen all day long to the likes of David Lloyd, Geoff Miller and Peter Parfitt.

When I think of the good rugby after-dinner speakers, then the late Gordon Brown, along with Willie John McBride would rank among the best. There must be something about second row forwards. I think the Gordon Brown story about Johan de Bruin, the player with the glass eye, is one of the funniest I've heard.

I'm sure this book will be a great success and that SPARKS will benefit. SPARKS is a charity founded by sportsmen and women that aims to give all children a healthy start in life. I am delighted to be associated with this book and the charity.

Bill Beaumont
September 2002

A

BEN AINSLIE

Olympic gold and silver medal holder for sailing. He is currently the World, European, National, Asia-Pacific and pre-Olympic champion in the Laser Class.

After the 1996 Olympics, I was asked to appear on Steve Redgrave's 'This is your Life'. I thought this was a bit odd as I had never met him. When we were introduced on the show Steve hadn't a clue who I was, but we managed to get through it with a quick handshake. It was my first time on a TV show and I don't think I made a very good impression!

* * *

My friend Iain Perey (a Sydney gold medallist) teamed up to sail a Laser 5000 (a very tricky-to-sail, double-handed, performance boat). It was our first day out and it was pretty windy. None of the other boats, including the top teams, went out as they thought the conditions were too rough.

Iain and I thought we would show them how it was done. We ended up wrecking the boat on a sand bar and having to be rescued by the RNLI. As we were towed ashore, all the competitors lined up to give us a clap. It was certainly the most embarrassing moment of my life.

JOHN ALDRIDGE

As a Liverpool striker he won the Division One championship in 1988, the Charity Shield in 1988 and the FA Cup in 1989. Aldridge also played for Newport County, Oxford United and Real Sociedad. He then became player/manager of Tranmere Rovers. Having made 882 appearances for club and country, John scored 474 goals overtaking Jimmy Greaves as British football's highest goal scorer. He was also capped 69 times for Ireland.

When having trials at Liverpool FC at the age of 14, I was told by Tom Saunders that I'd done well but the club would be giving me a phone call in the near future.

After signing for LFC eventually in 1987, I saw Tom (who was a lovely bloke) and said, 'I've waited 14 years for that phone call and it was a very costly one at that, £750,000.'

SAM ALLARDYCE

A former Bolton Wanderers player, then the manager at Limerick City, Notts County, Blackpool and Bolton Wanderers.

While manager of Limerick City I had to meet my chairman (Father Joe Young), along with the other directors in the local pub to find out if we had enough money for the wages for the players and myself. We often ran short so Joe would put his collar on, make a few phone calls and off we would go, collecting cash in all the pubs across the city until we had collected enough for the wages that week. We also had to raise the money for my flight from Bolton to Limerick. Truly a hand to mouth existence!

*   *   *

While I was manager of Bolton we set off to Arsenal with a late addition to our squad (Diawara) and I forgot to tell our kit man, who had not packed his shirt. When we arrived at Arsenal our kit man was in a tight spot, how to get another top?

With cunning initiative he went out on the street to look for a Bolton fan who was wearing one of our shirts. We managed to find a supporter and duly relieved him of his shirt. Then, we had to ask Arsenal if they would put his squad number and name on it. They kindly obliged. We drew the game 1–1 with ten men, Diawara coming on as sub.

As a small thank you to the fan, we presented him with a new shirt signed by all the players.

PETER ALLIS

Best known as the 'voice' of BBC golf, he was a former professional golfer who turned pro aged just 15, winning 20 European tournaments between 1954 and 1969. His first appearance in the Ryder Cup was in 1953, and with the exception of 1955 he represented Great Britain and Ireland in the event until 1969. He now enjoys a successful triple career as a broadcaster, writer and golf course design consultant.

An American gentleman was at St Andrews on his own, with no one to play with, so he takes the old caddie out. The weather was horrendous, blowing a gale, pouring rain.

At the 3rd hole the American goes into his golf bag, takes

out a bottle of whisky, and has a swig. The rain continues to lash down, terrible weather. Two holes later he has another swig. The course is deserted, not a soul in sight.

On the 8th, another swig, and again at the 10th. They turn for home, the wind changes so it is still against them, more rain, miles back to the clubhouse, he continues to have another swig.

Eventually on the 16th tee the American takes the bottle out and he says to the caddie, 'Is there not one single dry place on this godforsaken golf course?'

The old caddie replied, 'Aye sir, you could try the back of my throat.'

* * *

The late Dave Marr, who worked with me on both ABC Television and the BBC had some very good quotes:

'Trying to put one over on him is like the sun trying to sneak past a rooster.'

When referring to a hardened competitor who was keeping his match alive by sheer guts:

'Yep, he's a tough old dog to keep under the porch.'

22

DENNIS AMISS

England international cricketer from 1966 to 1977.
He scored over 100 first-class hundreds and had an
average of 46.

I wrote my first book during the 1974–75 England v Australia Test series in Australia. It was easy to write – Dennis Lillee and Jeff Thomson gave me plenty of time to write it.

* * *

Tony Greig loved to rile the opposition – it motivated him but it didn't do much for the rest of us except get us into trouble. I was batting at the Oval, England v West Indies, 1976. It was at the start of the series that Tony Greig said that we would make them grovel 3–0 down in the series.

So we were playing the last Test match in the series. It was a beautiful afternoon on a placid Oval wicket and Roberts, Holding, Holder and Daniel were tiring in the mid-afternoon heat – only one bouncer an over at about 85 m.p.h.

Suddenly a wicket fell and in came Tony Greig and as he met me he shouted at the top of his voice, 'I'm going to liven things up out here and get these West Indians going.'

They didn't need that. Just the sight of Tony made them bowl at 95 m.p.h., two to three bouncers an over – all hell broke out. All the time I was trying to quieten him down but it didn't make much difference.

After an over or two he lost his leg stump to a Michael Holding yorker. It's the only time I have been pleased to see an England captain out for nought. Afterwards it went back to normality – 85 m.p.h., one bouncer an over.

ROB ANDREW

An England rugby union international between 1985 and 1995, he won 71 caps and is England's most capped fly half. A Lions tourist in 1989 and 1993, he was a World Cup finalist in 1991. He also played first-class cricket for Nottinghamshire and is now Director of Rugby for the Newcastle Falcons.

In the build-up to the World Cup quarter-final against France in Paris in 1991, we were in our usual base at Versailles, just opposite the palace.

On the Friday before the match, we trained as usual at the Racing Club de France – a splendid venue, great facilities, good hospitality and a lovely lunch afterwards, all designed to lull us into a false sense of security.

Normally, following lunch, we would get on to the team coach and travel to the Parc des Princes to familiarise ourselves with the stadium. On this occasion, Jon Webb was our goal kicker and he had travelled ahead of the main party to do some kicking practice. As we arrived, I walked on to the pitch and over to Jon to ask him how it was going. 'Crap,' he said, 'The bastards won't give me the ball!'

MARCUS ARMYTAGE

The winner of the 1990 Grand National, riding Mr Frisk, Armytage was also a winner of the Kim Muir and National Hunt Chase (twice) at the Cheltenham Festival. Since retiring from the sport, he has become a successful journalist.

Training racehorses is often misconceived as a great occupation. At breakfast in a Lambourn yard one day an owner, who'd just seen his horse gallop against the backdrop of the Downs, the rising sun and larks singing, announced, 'If I ever win the Lottery I'm going to start training.'

'If I ever win the Lottery,' sighed his trainer, 'I'm going to stop training.'

*   *   *

The night before the Grand National a jockey returned to his hotel in the early hours with three less than attractive local Liverpool girls whom he had picked up in a nightclub. To him, in his state of inebriation, they looked like the first three home in the 1999 Miss World Contest. At the hotel door an avuncular doorman stopped the party. 'Come in, Sir,' he said, 'but I'm afraid you can't bring in your friends.'

The host pleaded for a full five minutes before he began to lose his patience. He demanded to know why his three new friends weren't allowed in with him.

'Because, Sir,' replied the doorman, 'you'll regret it in the morning.'

B

CHRIS BAILEY

— ◆ —

*A British Davis Cup tennis player from 1988 to 1993, he is
now a television presenter and commentator.*

I retired in 1996, and one of my first jobs is as a radio
commentator for Five Live. It is the Paris French Open Final –
Monica Seles v Arantxa Sanchez Vicario.

Well, all through championships the talk is of Kournikova
and other young beauties, how good it is for the game etc. As
for the final, Vicario wins.

With 15 seconds to hand back to London, the producer says,
'Say something punchy, that encapsulates whole tournament.'

I think quickly and wrap up: 'A great Vicario win – all the
talk may be of the young glamour babes coming through, but
just look at the podium, there is life in the old dogs yet.'

Oops…

*An England cricketer between 1949 and 1959. He played
62 Tests for England, including the successful 1953 Ashes
series against Australia, and is one of a select few cricketers
to have taken 100 wickets and scored 2,000 runs in Test
match cricket. Bailey scored over 20,000 runs and took over
2,000 wickets in his career. For 20 years he was the
Financial Times cricket and football correspondent, and he
was a regular Test match commentator for the BBC.*

Unlike the majority of former first-class cricketers, I am a very
very heavy handicap on any course. So, on the second occasion I
took part in the SPARKS Celebrity Golf Match at Bishop's
Stortford, I was delighted to find that I had been allocated the
same team that carried me the previous year without complaint.

During our happy, chatty second excursion, we encountered
a short hole with a very narrow gap to a green with well-
protected bunkers. My three colleagues immediately went into
a huddle and discussed the wind and whether to use a wedge,
nine or eight. I simply took my driver and aimed, hopefully,
for the breach. Like my driving, my eyesight was also much
shorter than that of the rest of my side, but I did just about see
my ball find its way onto the green. My team-mates, however,
were able to watch, and then to cheer, as it made its way
towards the little hole. The noise when it went in was not only
deafening, but was the signal for exuberant 'high fives' – a
method of celebrating, like embracing and removing one's
shirt, that became popular long after my playing career. Mind
you, five points did help our score.
　Everyone at the club that day became aware of what happened as the shot was also a 'nearest the pin hole' and Gary
Lineker presented me with the prize at dinner that evening. I

apologised to the large gathering for not buying them all a drink, explaining that I never went to golf carrying over £200 in cash, or credit cards, while, clearly, it would surely have been wrong of me to tempt anyone to drink and drive. Having been forgiven, I was able to find an old England touring blazer, which was raffled for SPARKS the following year. It was certainly a day I shall never forget.

CLARE BALDING

A former champion amateur lady jockey who is currently a BBC sports broadcaster. She fronts all of the racing coverage and presents high-profile equestrian events such as Badminton, Burghley and Gatcombe. She also works for Radio Five Live and writes a weekly sports column for the Evening Standard.

A renowned racehorse trainer was once asked to address a group of well-educated schoolgirls at an evening seminar at their school. A very private and shy man, he was alleged to have had sleepless nights preceding the event.

It was a long time since he had been at school and he had no idea of what would be required to hold their interest. If he was too technical about his subject, he might bore them to sleep. On the other hand he did not wish to patronise them.

In a state of panic, he rang Lester Piggott; surely the great man had had to endure many such evenings and he would be just the man to ask how to approach the ensuing ordeal.

'Lester, I've got to do a talk to a group of schoolgirls on Thursday night. Whatever shall I tell them?'

'I should tell them that you've got flu!' came the reply.

IAN BALDING

A racehorse trainer who has trained over 2,000 winners, including victories in 41 Group One races, 33 Group Two races, 49 Group Three races and a further 60 Listed races. The most famous horse trained though, must be Mill Reef, who won the Derby, the King George at Ascot and the Arc de Triomphe. Ian also played rugby union for Bath and Newbury and won a rugby blue at Cambridge.

Some years ago I was asked if I would help out with a group of racing enthusiasts from Radley College who were having a post-A-level outing to Windsor races. The master in charge of the outing was none other than the Warden himself, Dennis Silk, and he as much as any of his pupils was desperate to make the trip a profitable one.

As I informally addressed the boys on the steps of the weighing room, I spotted Willie Carson about to weigh out for the first race. I was keen to spread the liability and asked him if he could give the eager racegoers a minute of his time. The inevitable question was asked:

'What's going to win the first race Willie?' There was a silence as he looked frantically at his race card for inspiration.

'Hold on a second and I'll ask the other jockeys, they'll have more of an idea,' was the reply. He disappeared back into the weighing room before returning with a large grin. 'Apparently, I will!'

He duly did, at rewarding odds, to the great delight of the Warden and his pupils.

IAIN BALSHAW

An England rugby union international full back during the 2001 Six Nations Championship. Despite the famous comments by Finlay Calder, who said, 'If Iain Balshaw is an international full back, then I'm Mel Gibson,' Balshaw's five tries in four matches that year earned him rave reviews. Balshaw was a Lions tourist on the 2001 tour of Australia.

A rugby referee died and went to heaven. Stopped by St Peter at the gates, he was told that only brave people who had performed heroic deeds and had the courage of their convictions could enter. If the ref could describe a situation in his life where he had shown all these characteristics, he would be allowed in.

'Well,' said the ref, 'I was reffing a game between England and Australia at Twickenham. Australia were four points ahead, with one minute to go. The England wing made a break, passed the ball inside to his lock, the lock was driven on by his forwards, he passed the ball out to his flanker who ducked under the despairing tackles and went over in the corner. However, the flanker dropped the ball before he could ground it, but as England were clearly the better side all game, I ruled that he had grounded the ball legally, and so awarded the try.'

'OK, that was fairly brave of you, but I will have to check the facts in the book,' said St Peter, and disappeared off to look it up. He came back and said, 'Sorry, but there is no record of this. Can you help me to trace it? When did it happen?'

The ref looks at his watch and replied, 'About 45 seconds ago!'

GORDON BANKS

A former England goalkeeper and part of the 1966 World Cup-winning side. He also played for Leicester City and Stoke City.

When playing at Hampden Park for Scotland at an inter-nation competition, we were provided with two bags to carry all our kit. Unfortunately both were exactly the same. In one bag were the indispensable tools of a footballer's trade, my boots, perfectly fitting, crucial to my success on the field. I though, picked up the wrong bag. The bus had parked up, we were quite a way to the changing rooms when I suddenly realised to my horror – I had the wrong bag and so no boots!

Jack Charlton came to the rescue and kindly said I could borrow a pair of his.

The only thing wrong was the size. He was 11 and I was 9½. Alf Ramsey was aware of the situation by now, and sent the trainer to find the bus and dig around to try and find my correct bag.

Time was ticking, it was getting near the signal for us to walk out.

I was wading around the dressing room in these boots and looking like Coco the Clown. I was nervous, how was I to perform with these great oversized boots on?

Fortunately, just before running out the trainer came sprinting in, with the correct bag over his shoulder to save the day at the last moment.

On went my size 9½s – much better!

JACK BANNISTER

*A former Warwickshire cricketer, he played 368 matches
for his county between 1950 and 1968, taking over 1,000
first-class wickets.*

Glenn McGrath is bowling for Worcestershire and bounces and
hits the Nottinghamshire no. 11 at Trent Bridge in 2000. The
crowd barracks him as the twelfth man, Richard Stemp, comes
on with a glass of water.

McGrath yells, 'That's why you whingeing Poms will always
be losers.'

Stemp replies to McGrath, 'If it hadn't been for us whingeing
Poms, you lot would've been speaking German now.'

STUART BARNES

*An England Rugby Union fly half between 1984 and 1993,
he was a Lions tourist in 1993, and is now a Sky TV
commentator and analyst.*

Miles Harrison, Sky's lead commentator, during England v
Ireland: 'Wood has been penalised for going down on the
England hooker.'

Me, holding back my mirth: 'No, that's terrible, you cannot
go down on a hooker on the field of play, Miles.'

Harrison, listening, drops the microphone, giving 30 blessed
seconds of relief for those viewers who missed Harrison's
Colemanballs.

* * *

Richard Hill, self-styled hard man of English back play is on as a substitute for Nigel Melville, whom the All Blacks somehow confused with a doormat. Nigel somehow confused a ripped shirt and a bloodied back with a strained hamstring. Looking back to that day in Wellington, 1985, I don't blame him now. Anyway, Hill – yes. The man known as 'Rouge Tête' was heavily engaged in what was an epic of its kind, a 28-man punch-up.

He went for a teenage wing called John Kirwan. Alas for Hill, JK could box almost as well as he played Test match rugby. I was lying on the floor, wrestling with the smallest All Black (Steve Pokere), but the two of us broke up our handbagging to watch JK land several jabs on the chin of the hapless Hill, who, far from going down, merely retreated from what was, on the television screen, far right to off stage left.

Bruised egos and bruised chins, Hilly boy.

MARTIN BAYFIELD

———— • ◆ • ————

*A former England rugby union international, earning 61
caps between 1991 and 1996, the 6'10" lock was also a
Lions tourist in 1993.*

While in the police I was helping in the search of a known drug dealer's house. The man also happened to be a raging homosexual. While searching downstairs I heard roars of laughter from upstairs. My sergeant, crying with laughter ran down to get me. In the man's bedroom all around me they were crying, screaming with hysterical laughter. Why? Because there above his bed was a poster of me!

A former England rugby union international lock between 1975 and 1982, winning 34 caps. He captained England to the 1980 Grand Slam and the Lions during their tour to South Africa in 1980.

England were playing Australia in 1982. Leading at half-time, I had my back to the old South Stand at Twickenham. I was giving my usual boring team talk, but noticed that I was gradually losing the attention of my team-mates. Eventually, they were all peering over my shoulder, jostling for position to see what it was.

It was of course Miss Erica Roe making her first appearance at Twickenham, livening up what was otherwise quite a boring game. Still I hadn't turned around until Peter Wheeler, the England hooker, shouted across, 'Bill, you are going to have to look at this, some bird has run on to the pitch with your arse on her chest.'

Selected for the full British ski team at the age of 15 and
competed on the World Cup tour between 1981 and 1995.
He represented Great Britain at four Winter Olympic
Games and five World Championships. His eighth-place
position in the 1988 Olympic Downhill at Calgary remains
a British Olympic record for a male skier. He has also
notched up four overall British Championship titles.

One of the most important members of the British ski team's back-up crew is the video man. He films the training runs or races each day, so that the racers' technique can be meticulously studied every evening. Usually this is a voluntary post, performed by a young ex-racer or ski instructor who wants to travel the world for a couple of seasons and gain some coaching experience. But when I was racing with the team, there seemed to be a jinx on the poor guy. Our first video man to run into trouble was Johnny Vaitkus, a former racer from Edinburgh, who worked for the team during 1987.

One afternoon in Wengen, a few days prior to the classic Lauberhorn Downhill, our coach decided that we would do a ski-testing session – up on the Mannlichen part of the mountain, for those of you who know Wengen. All went well, and at 4 p.m., we started queuing to ride the cable-car down, which was the only way back down to the village – or so we thought! Suddenly Johnny grunted, 'Forget this queue, I'm skiing down,' and set off down the precarious slopes below the cable-car station. He soon vanished from sight. When we had finally negotiated the queue and ridden down, we returned to our hotel, expecting to see Johnny relaxing in his room, but there was no sign of him. Half an hour later, one of the team walkie-talkies sprang to life: 'Hey guys, can you look up the mountain and check whether there's a cliff below me!'

By now it was dusk, but when we looked up towards the Mannlichen, we could just make out a tiny figure, perched above a large cliff.

'Yes Johnny, there's a cliff, you'll have to walk back up and find another route!'

He did so, taking a route which led him close to one of the big pylons that carry the cable-car. At that moment, as we watched from far below, the descending cable-car stopped at the pylon, and the lift operator climbed out, gesturing down to Johnny to climb up the pylon and get into the cable-car. We watched Johnny do this, returned to the hotel and expected to see him in a few minutes. But it was two more hours before he reappeared, looking very sheepish. Apparently, the lift operators had dragged him off to the police station. There, he had been neither charged nor fined, but given such a severe dressing-down that he was very subdued for the remainder of the week! He had found his vocation though and moved to Chamonix to become an 'extreme' skier, appearing in photoshoots. One time he nearly died, when stranded alone with a broken leg in a remote valley. But so far he has survived!

The British team's next video man, recruited by my brother Graham and myself, was a friend of ours from Harrogate – a ski instructor at the local dry ski slope. Although his real name was Alistair Grant, he soon became nicknamed 'the Wookie' because of his swept-back hairdo and his playful attitude. This attitude was severely tested at the 1989 World Championships at Vail and Beaver Creek. He had been instructed by our Austrian coach to climb up a tree with the video camera, as this would afford the best vantage point from which to film the most difficult section of the downhill course. Unfortunately, just as he began filming, the branch upon which he was standing broke. Later, in the knowledge that the Wookie was only bruised, we derived great entertainment from watching the tape – a loud crack, followed by lots of bumps and 'ows' as various branches sped past the camera in an upwards direction. Our coach was very relieved that the camera was not damaged. Later that week, the Wookie's bad luck was to continue. While out on the town in Vail, he started dancing with a short blonde girl. After chatting to her for a while, he seemed to lose interest. (Afterwards he claimed, 'She was too short.') Our team manager, Ian Mackenzie, questioned the Wookie the next morning, when Alistair revealed, 'Oh, she said she was some kind of actress, said she'd been Goose's wife in *Top Gun*, but I've never heard of her.'

'You idiot,' said Ian, 'you just turned your nose up at Meg Ryan!'

NIGEL BENN

Nicknamed 'The Dark Destroyer', Benn is a legend in British boxing. He was the Commonwealth middleweight champion, the WBO middleweight champion in 1990 and the WBC super middleweight champion from 1992 to 1996. Benn was one of the most dangerous and explosive boxers of the 1980s and 1990s.

Fighting Chris Eubank for the first time in 1990 was hard enough. He was unbeaten, arrogant and I hated him with a passion. But when I got on the scales I was 5½ pounds over. That's a huge amount of weight to shift ... and that's when the weigh-ins were on the same day as the fight. So on the day of my hardest ever fight, I had to go on a three-mile run, sauna, steam room, to skip, go for a bike ride, back in the sauna, more skipping and a third visit to the sauna ... all before the fight.

When I arrived at the NEC two hours before the fight, I was physically and emotionally shattered. And then we fought each other to a standstill. But I will never use it as an excuse. I was beaten by the better man. But I hated him more for what he made me go through in the most gruelling 12 hours of my life.

The irony of the tale is that Chris and I now go to the gym together!

JOHN BENTLEY

An England rugby union international winger between 1988 and 1997, he was also a Lions tourist to South Africa in 1997. He also played rugby league for Halifax and Leeds.

While touring SA with the British Lions in 1997, I had the misfortune of rooming with Keith Wood for 11 days in Pretoria. As a result of his position, hooker, his shoulders are knackered. When retiring to bed, at approx 9.30 p.m., he can only sleep in one position. He props two pillows under both shoulders in order to drop off. From the second he closes his eyes he begins to snore. Having gone seven nights without getting any sleep, I was fed up and took advice from the team doctor.

As he fell asleep on the eighth night, I reached over onto his bed and kissed his cheek. He spent the three remaining nights propped up in the corner of his bed waiting to see what I'd do next. There was only one man awake after that and it wasn't me!

An award-winning comedian and after-dinner speaker,
Soccer Speaker of the Year and goalkeeper for the
Old Wilsonians 7th XI.

At half-time the captain came up to me and said, 'I'd like a word with you about the second half.'

I said, 'What about it?'

He said, 'Would you like a wall for the kick-off?'

* * *

Whenever I met the late, great and much-missed Bobby Moore, he would always ask me about my game. He would say, 'Play Saturday?' and I would regale him, in some detail, with my exploits.

But once I met him at the end of the week so he changed the tense of his enquiry. He said, 'Playing Saturday?'

I said, 'I'm captain!'

He said, 'Do you think you'll catch the coin?'

HAROLD BIRD

*Arguably the most famous umpire in the history of cricket,
he was first a player for Yorkshire and Leicestershire. As an
umpire he officiated at over 150 international matches, and
is, even after retirement, an eccentric and much-loved
character within the game.*

There are, unfortunately, many reasons as to why play may be
delayed or indeed stopped altogether: rain, bad light, injuries,
a misshapen ball and the like, but there are one or two that are
quite unique ...

England v West Indies – I was umpiring, the match was in full
swing, the crowd was buzzing. A titanic struggle as always
between bat and ball. Unfortunately out of necessity, I stopped
play, gathered the batsmen and the captain of the fielding side
to me and said, 'I am sorry gentlemen, but nature calls,' and off
I went to the changing rooms. Luckily the players were hugely
amused and as soon as the crowd clicked, I received a huge
roar from them.

※　※　※

Who would ever forget Dennis Lillie, the great Australian fast
bowler, loved by his team–mates, respected by all, and feared
by many, myself included.

I receive all sorts of things from bowlers, hats, sweaters and
the like but on this occasion Lillie put a snake in my pocket. I
ran over the ground to shake the snake from my pocket, to the
amusement of the players. Out it flew, at last, to my relief, only
to lie still on the grass.

Only then did I realise WHY it was lying so still. It was, of
course, a rubber one.

MARK BLUNDELL

A former Formula One and Indycar driver, who has also won the Le Mans 24 Hour Endurance race, Mark is now an ITV Formula One analyst.

In 1991 myself and Martin Brundle were team-mates in the Brabham F1 team. It was my first year in F1 and we were travelling from Japan to Australia – about a nine-hour trip. I arrived at the airport early, checked in, and to my surprise found that I had been upgraded from economy to first class for the flight. I thought, 'Great, being an F1 Driver is so cool!'

As I found out later, Blundell and Brundle are pronounced and spelt the same Japanese, hence I had been given Martin Brundle's first-class seat instead of my economy seat!

I sat up front, got settled in looking forward to the trip in comfort when a Japanese Airline stewardess came up to me: 'Excuse me, Sir, could you move please, there has been a mistake!' At this point Martin is standing in the doorway of the airplane, furious, nodding his head for me to move!

I, of course, took advantage of the Japanese people being so polite and refused to move, pointing out that I had been given this seat and was going to stay there.

Of course, the lady obliged by letting 'Brundell san' remain in his nice first-class seat; Martin was told he would have to stay in economy. He was MAD! He'd paid for his first-class seat only for me to be sitting in it. He did not talk to me for a while, but we now laugh about it.

One of many things Martin and I have had fun with, having similar names!

SIR MICHAEL BONALLACK

Amateur golf champion and former Secretary of the
Royal & Ancient Golf Club.

An old married couple, no longer able to play a full round of golf, still managed a round on the putting green every day, following which they both dozed off to sleep in chairs on the club verandah. One day the old girl woke up, picked up her putter and whacked her sleeping husband across the shins. Startled, he woke up.

'What's that for?'

'Fifty years of lousy sex.'

Back they both went to sleep. This time, he woke up, grabbed his putter and whacked her across her shins.

'What's that about?' she asked.

'For knowing the difference!!!'

RICHARD BOXALL

A golf professional who played on the European Tour for an
unbroken 16 years. He hit the headlines in 1991 when,
while in contention for the Open at Royal Birkdale, he frac-
tured his leg while driving at the 9th hole of the third round.
He is now a Sky TV golf analyst.

I was working for Sky on the Australian golf, the Heineken Classic at the Vines, Perth. I had just started doing studio work and commentary for Sky and the presenter Andrew Castle and I had to talk over the action that was going on.

Nick O'Hearne had played a par three and had pushed it left. He was stuck behind a tree and had an advertising sign in the way. He tried to get a drop but didn't get one. Nick walks in and takes the stance as if to play it left-handed.

Andrew asks me, 'What do you think he's doing?'

'It looks to me as if he's going to be really brave and take the shot left-handed,' I said.

To which Andrew replies, 'Nick is left-handed, Richard.'

Sky still take the Mick out of me to this day.

KYRAN BRACKEN

An England rugby union international scrum half, he has won 41 caps to date, and was a 1997 Lions tourist to South Africa.

It was back in 1997 and as a promotion for the Tetley's Bitter Cup Final, my flatmate, Danny Grewcock, decided to stitch me up on Sky TV. He invited the cameras around to our flat when I wasn't around and kitted the TV room out with every single bit of Bracken memorabilia he could find. The dining table had place-mats with my face on, the walls were covered with photos of me and my international shirts lay spread across the sofas. Every inch of the room had been covered as if it was a shrine to me.

He then proceeded to be interviewed for the forthcoming game in the room, explaining it was difficult to live with me and my self-indulgence. You can imagine how embarrassed I was when I found out and walked in on them.

People still ask me if my lounge is the same today.

* * *

Revenge was sweet. Two weeks later I rang Sky. We pretended the team were all going to wear Saracens sand-storming suits as a promotion for the game.

Hook, line and sinker. Grewcock was equipped with the big turban, the Saracens sword and Sahara trousers. He was given his instructions. He growled into the camera saying, 'COME –

WATCH THE MIGHTY SARACENS SANDSTORMERS TAKE ON THE WASPS.'

He then growled again.

His mobile phone then went off. I was on the end of the line: 'Danny, I think that's quits!'

It was great satisfaction when I saw the reaction on his face. Jeremy Beadle, eat your heart out!!

MIKE BREARLEY

A former England cricketer between 1976 and 1981, he is known as one of England's finest captains. He was once described as 'having a degree in people', such were his motivational skills. A former captain of Middlesex, he played 39 Tests at an average of 22, and hit 25,185 first class runs, averaging over 37 with a top score of 312 not out. After retirement he has combined his career as a psychotherapist with occasional cricket journalism.

Bodyline series, 1932–33 – the last Test at Sydney. Douglas Jardine, fielding close in, is whacked on the shin. The blood seeps down over his boot. Jardine doesn't bother to inspect the wound, stands unflinching. At the end of the over, Harold Larwood says to him, 'Skip, you'd better go off and have that looked at.'

Jardine: 'What? And let 50,000 convicts know I'm hurt?'

* * *

From the days of amateurs and professionals at cricket. Lord's, the first day of Fred Titmus's debut for Middlesex. Soon after the start, an announcment comes over the loudspeakers: 'Ladies and gentlemen, a correction to your scorecards. For "F J Titmus" read "Titmus F J".'

An England cricketer between 1984 and 1989, he is one of three Englishmen to have scored successive centuries against Australia.

I was walking through a graveyard the other day and came across a headstone that read, 'Here lies a journalist, a true and honest man.'

I thought to myself, 'That's strange, burying two people in one grave!'

* * *

Two Irishmen were walking home along a road after a night in the pub. One of them trips over a stone on the side of the road. He turns round and sees it's got writing on. He reads it and says to his friend, 'Hey Paddy, we must have walked into a graveyard. There's a chap here that died aged 72.'

Paddy says, 'What was his name?'

'Miles from Dublin!'

"So you're claiming unfair dismissal"

TIM BROOKE-TAYLOR

A former director at Derby County and President of
SPARKS in 1996, he is a renowned actor and broadcaster.

You don't have to be a great sportsman to have a great sporting moment, but you do need to be a wannabe great sportsman.

In pro-celebrity golf tournaments there are moments, brief moments admittedly, when you really feel you've made the grade; you haven't, of course, but it feels great.

It was the pro-am of the Dunhill Masters at Woburn and I was on the tee with my two other amateurs, waiting for our professional to arrive. Five minutes to go and still no pro. Suddenly, a young lady from Dunhill rushes up and says, 'You're playing with Ballas Truss.'

Ballas Truss? Ballas Truss? Oh Ballesteros. BALLESTEROS! Seve Ballesteros, my hero.

I had mixed feelings. I wanted to play with him, but not in front of such a huge crowd. (Mixed feelings, by the way, always used to be, 'Seeing your mother-in-law driving your brand new car over a cliff'.)

I got so nervous that I cut my hand trying to get the ball out of my bag. I then heard a voice: 'Tim' would you mind having your photo taken with Seve?' Would I mind!? Is the Pope Catholic? Stupid question.

The photographer very kindly gave me a copy of this photo and I have a portrait-sized version of it in my home.

We were playing a Texas Scramble. Everyone drives off and all four of us play our second shots from the best-placed ball. We used my drive on the first. *My* drive! (All right, so the other two amateurs went left and right into the woods of Woburn like the Red Arrows and Seve hit his a mile, but unfortunately behind a tree. And *I* topped mine 150 yards down the middle – but it was down the middle.)

We used my second as well – topped onto the green. I had been in awe of Seve, but now he was a passenger. Yes, yes I should have known. On the fourth hole he hit the best shot I've ever seen. 'Great shot Sev,' I said. Yes I actually said 'Sev'.

He turned with a well-placed look of contempt on his face, 'No ees no a gray sho. Eeesa good but eesa no gray.' I suddenly realised I'd stepped out of line and had for a brief, mad moment thought I was the god. He's a nice man Seve and, realising I was upset, said kindly, 'You must remember, Tom [not great with names though], I maybe heet two or three great shots a week.'

Come the last hole and Seve (by now Mr Ballesteros, Sir) has hit a wonderful drive. It's a par five and as I've got nothing to lose I get out my driver. For once the god of golf was really with me and I hit the ball 250 yards to within 10 feet of the hole. I'd done this in front of a huge crowd and in front of my god. Seve said 'Good shot Teem.'

And *I* said, and I truly meant it, 'No, I'm sorry Seve, *that* was a GREAT shot.' And it was. But you must remember that I only hit one or two great shots in my life.

DOUGIE BROWN

———————— ◆ ————————

An England international cricketer who has played nine One Day Internationals for his country, he made his debut against India in the Champions Trophy in Sharjah during the 1997–98 season. Brown is an all-rounder and plays for Warwickshire.

I was fielding on the boundary during a one-day game v Surrey, directly in front of the Committee area. Former Prime Minister John Major was sitting directly behind me and I was making pleasantries in between deliveries, wondering if I was going to make an impressive catch in front of him.

At that, Ben Hollioake launched one out to me on the boundary, where I got beautifully into position. My usually dependable hands for some reason did not work, and the ball hit me flush on the forehead, bouncing 30 metres into the sightscreen. I turned to try and hide my embarrassment, only to catch Mr Major belly-laughing into his phone ...

I had made an impression on him, but not quite as intended!

* * *

We were fielding in the slips and the conversation between balls for some reason turned to opera. Keith Piper, our quirky little wicketkeeper, astounded us all by saying that his Granny used to take him to the opera as a kid. Two words you would certainly not use together are Piper and opera!

'Which one?' The lads asked.

'Em, Em, I can't remember!' replied Keith.

'Was it *Madame Butterfly*? *Carmen*?' After various stabs at what it could have been, there was a spark in Piper's brain and we stood with bated breath ...

'I got it. It were *Dick Whittington*!!!'

The game was delayed for a moment or two while we picked ourselves off our knees and dried our eyes!

KEN BROWN

❖

A Ryder Cup golf player on five occasions and now a
BBC commentator.

Commentating on Nick Faldo and his caddy Fanny Sunneson lining up shots at the Scottish Open: 'Some weeks Nick likes to use Fanny; other weeks he prefers to do it himself.'

PAUL BURKE

❖

An Ireland rugby union international fly half who
made his debut against England in 1995. Burke has scored
105 points in 11 appearances for his country.

I was playing for Cardiff against arch rivals Newport at Cardiff Arms Park during the 1999–2000 season, when the most extraordinary thing happened to me. We had just scored a try in the corner in the dying minutes of the game and needed the conversion for victory. It was a nerve-wracking moment. All went quiet for this crucial moment in the match. It was all up to me and I knew it.

I prepared to take the conversion from the touchline. Being a goal kicker, my own personal routine is very important, so I placed the ball onto the carefully-constructed pile of sand, I walked back, looked up at the posts and steadied myself, deep in concentration, totally focused on the job in hand. I had no idea what was about to happen.

To my amazement, a drunken Newport supporter leapt over

50

the advertising boards, sprinted over to where I was and kicked my teed-up ball clean off the sand. It sailed high into the stands – a pretty impressive effort.

Huge cheers followed, as the policemen, stewards and even the referee (who was an ex-policeman) struggled to apprehend this over-eager Newport supporter. I collected the ball, and went back to building my sand tee, with my concentration somewhat shattered.

After a couple of minutes of rolling about in the mud, the supporter was removed to the biggest cheer of the night.

Ironically, as the fan's drunken attempt was a good one, the pressure was really on. I placed the ball on the sand, took a furtive glance at the crowd, stepped back and, thankfully, managed to caress the ball though the posts – victory for Cardiff and, for me, five seconds of fame on 'A Question of Sport'!

C

JONATHAN CALLARD

A former England rugby union international full back, he holds the Bath club record for the most points (1,175), and is a former Bath Director of Rugby.

Bath were due to play Llanelli in the Heineken Cup European quarter-final. The match had already been postponed once due to heavy rain, which had not stopped for three days.

The players were asked to leave the hotel and walk to the ground, which was ten minutes away. The rain was lashing down. Half-way to the ground, Mark Regan stopped and shouted to the rest of the team, 'It's alright, it has stopped raining.'

It hadn't stopped raining, he was just walking under a bridge.

OLLIE CAMPBELL

A former Republic of Ireland rugby international fly half between 1974 and 1984, he won 22 caps and was a Lions tourist in 1980 and 1983.

Moss Keane is probably the most loved and adored Irish sporting personality of his or any generation. This was probably best encapsulated a few years ago when 250 people were invited to his surprise 50th birthday party. It is no exaggeration to say that in fact over 500 people actually turned up!

There are many stories about Moss [some of which are even true!]. Here is a very small personal selection.

When asked to say a few words at very short notice at a luncheon in Ballymore in Brisbane before Ireland played Tonga in the first World Cup in 1987, he stood up and in his unique Kerry accent, began by saying that he felt like a dog surrounded by four trees – he didn't have a leg to stand on!

Throughout most of his career [in the old amateur days] Moss lived by the dictum that moderate drinkers live longer – and it served them bloody well right!

On the week before probably the most important game of his career when Ireland were due to play Scotland at Lansdowne Road, with the opportunity of winning the Triple Crown for the first time in 33 years, Moss decided to make the ultimate sacrifice and cut his drink in half – so he left out the water. [It worked and we won!]

After many years of persuasion by his wife Ann, for peace's sake, Moss decided to join Alcoholics Anonymous. Ever since he has been drinking under an assumed name!

A French rugby union international, he has gained 35 caps
to date. Castaignede has played at fly half, centre and full
back for his country and plays club rugby for Saracens.

There are times when international rugby is deadly serious but, as you can imagine, when a group of boys get together for long periods, some individuals get up to some mischief.

One Monday, before an international match which was to be played on the following Saturday, our prop, Christian Califano, was in a cheeky mood.

At training there are bananas available at all times. Califano had just eaten one and had the skin in his hand. Not having a bin nearby, he saw our second row's boots lying nearby. (Now, this huge 6'6" giant went by the name of Olivier Merle. He was massive and had a temper too.) Califano quietly walked over and slipped the banana skin into one of the boots.

There was no reaction all week from Olivier. Not a whisper. The reason? Olivier had two pairs of boots; one pair for training and another *special* pair he only wore for matches. Califano, of course, had sabotaged Olivier's pristine, clean match boots. Olivier had not worn them so he hadn't found the banana skin. The problem was, no one else realised. Everybody thought he'd found the boots, and just not mentioned the offending fruit.

This was not your average international. This was the Grand Slam decider against Scotland in 1997. The training had gone well all week. Everybody was hugely up for it. The banana skin, meanwhile, continued to fester and congeal in Merle's left boot.

We all went out onto the pitch, warmed up, and came back into the changing rooms. Five minutes before kick-off, we were all concentrating when there was a huge roar. It was Olivier, who had finally put on his match boots. Squelch went the decaying banana skin as the slippery, sticky mess oozed into his sock and squirted out of his boot.

Califano instantly paled as he realised what he had done and immediately attempted to apologise. Olivier, though, was having none of it and furiously chased Califano around the changing rooms. The rest of us eventually stopped Merle, shouting, 'We have a game in five minutes!'

The crowd gave us a huge cheer as we ran out, Califano sprinted onto the pitch, and Olivier Merle sprinted after him. The crowd, of course, thought we were just very focused on the game. Little did they know why these two looked so pumped up – Califano through fear, and Merle through anger!

MIKE CATT

*An England rugby union international, he has won 56 caps
to date and has played in every back-line position for his
country except scrum half. He was a Lions tourist in
1997 and 2001.*

A man has a ticket for the Rugby World Cup final but is seated right at the top of the stand, in the corner, with the worst possible view of the pitch. As the match starts he notices one empty seat, beautifully positioned, bang on the half-way line, about ten rows back. Taking a chance, he scurries all the way down from the top of the stand, to where the spare seat is.

'Excuse me, Sir,' he says to the man sitting next to the empty seat. 'Is anyone sitting there?'

'No,' replies the man. 'That seat is empty.'

'That's incredible, who in their right mind would have a seat like this for the World Cup final, the biggest sporting event in rugby and not use it?'

'Well, actually the seat belongs to me,' replies the seated man. 'I was supposed to come with my wife but she passed away.'

'Oh, I'm sorry to hear that. That's terrible, but couldn't you find someone else – a friend or even a neighbour to take the seat?' The seated man shakes his head.

'They've all gone to the funeral.'

CRAIG CHALMERS

───────────── • ◆ • ─────────────

A former Scotland rugby union international fly half, he gained 60 caps between 1989 and 1999. He helped Scotland to win the 1990 Grand Slam and was a Lions tourist to Australia in 1989.

1990, I was in Hong Kong for the world-famous 7s tournament, playing for the Scottish Borderers and, as you do when on the trip, we were in a pub called the Go Down, getting stuck into a few beers. Across the room was Will Carling whom I had not seen since we had beaten England in the famous Grand Slam game at Murrayfield earlier in the season. Anyway, I took no notice as I happened to be chatting to the owner's daughter, just being friendly, and we were engrossed in conversation.

Meanwhile at the bar, Mickey Skinner [Skins] and Will Carling were busy having a game of spoof. Carling lost. His penalty? He walked up and chucked a full bucket of water and ice all over me – I was a mess. Only one thing to do, swear revenge.

'I'll get you Carling, I don't know when but I'll get you.' Lots of laughter all around and all was apparently forgotten.

Well, the week went by and it was the Sunday after the 7s. The English boys were on stage in the hotel, and did an act as many teams did, doing a spoof Miss World sketch, with make-up – the lot. After the sketch they raced upstairs to get changed for the night out.

Down came Carling, all chinos, beautifully pressed shirt, carefully combed mane, ready for the evening ahead. Skins though, had got down first (naturally) and had two jugs of lager nearby. I wandered over.

'Do you mind if I borrow those, Skins?' I asked.

'No problem, mate.'

Now armed, I sauntered over to Carling, who was busy looking in the other direction, and unloaded these two jugs all over him.

Did he lose his cool? No, full marks, he took it in good grace.

Respect, for the first time ever, from a Scotsman!

DARREN CLARKE

A golfer from Northern Ireland who has been a Ryder Cup team member in 1997, 1999 and 2003, Clarke represented Ireland in both the World Cup from 1994 to 1996 and the Alfred Dunhill Cup from 1994 to 1999. He represented Great Britain and Ireland in the inaugural 2000 Seve Ballesteros Trophy and has many other tournament victories to his name.

Tom Weiskopf once said: 'In golf, when you play well, you never understand how you ever played badly. When you play badly, you never understand how you ever played well.'

I was 'best man' in West Palm Beach seven years ago on New Year's Eve and found out that weddings are a bit different in America …. It just happened that it was quite a wait for the best man to recount his tales. We started drinking in the afternoon, one thing led to another, as it does in a celebration and at last at 11.45 p.m. it was time for me – the best man – to close the deal on a wonderful day. The trouble was, I was nervous … and hammered.

Only one thing for it, I grabbed the mike, determined to make a strong start to get everyone's attention.

'Llllllladd'ss an' G'tllll'mmmn'enn.'

I got no further. Over I fell – backwards, straight into the band, who were all prepared to help the guests dance the night away. I demolished it – totally.

'S'rry 'bout that,' and continued my speech. I started talking quickly, and as always when I am pissed, spoke in a broad Irish accent.

The guests, half-American, half-Irish – couldn't understand a word.

The moral? – Don't drink when you're best man. One more thing, don't stand in front of the band.

BEN COHEN

*An England rugby union international winger, he has
18 caps so far and was a Lions tourist to
Australia in 2001.*

Northampton Saints have a proud history. It is a wonderful club that tends to inspire loyalty from its players and fans alike. One such player who is very much part of the fabric of Northampton's recent history, a club stalwart, goes by the name of Harvey Thorneycroft.

Harvey is a great organiser of charity events and tours. One time, he had organised a Northampton tour to Africa and all were aboard the BA flight, fully prepared to spread the rugby gospel. The plane took off and everyone was settling into their seats, when Harvey piped up, 'Bloody hell, my ears are killing me.' Now this caused a snigger or two as he is well-renowned as having one of the finest sets of lugholes on the circuit.

'Seriously lads, it's the pressure, anyone know what to do?'

Tim Rodber [Rodders], who was sitting nearby, gave the standard reply that everyone who has travelled knows: 'What you do Harv, is hold your nose and blow. That will equalise the pressure and you'll feel fine.'

'OK, here goes.' Harvey went quiet, concentrated, held his nose and blew out: 'Wwwwwwshhhhhh.'

'It's no good lads, I've still got it,' he said turning to his mates, who to his bewilderment, were all doubled up with laughter.

'No, you muppet,' said Rodders. 'When you blow out, you have to keep your mouth closed as well!'

A Welsh international footballer playing for Fulham FC. He started his career with Manchester City as a trainee before moving back to Wales with Swansea City. He was ruled out of a large part of the 2000–2001 season when he broke his leg in three places in a horrific car crash at the turn of the year. Coleman finally returned to action in May 2002 when playing in Wales' 1–0 win over Germany at the Millennium Stadium. He has also played for Blackburn Rovers.

While I was playing for Crystal Palace, we were 3–0 down at half time and the manager Alan Smith flew into a rage during our team talk. Sitting next to me was my team-mate Richard Shaw, and next to him was a table with tea and sandwiches on it.

During his moment of anger Alan Smith threw a cup of tea at the wall and up-turned the tray of sandwiches, one of which landed on Richard's head. He was so afraid, he sat there for ten minutes with the sandwich still on top of his head until Alan left the room!

* * *

During the same team talk our goalkeeper Woody (Andrew Woodman) was coming in for a bit of stick from Alan, who unstrapped his gold Rolex watch from his wrist and dangled it in front of Woody, saying, 'You'll never own one of these son, because after a performance like that, you'll never go any further in the game.'

With that he lobbed the watch at Woody to catch, who nervously dropped it on the floor!

TERRY CONROY

*A former Republic of Ireland international, who won
26 caps; he also played for Stoke City.*

In 1969, Stoke City had a player named Roy Vernon. He had played for Everton, captained Wales and he was coming to the end of his career. He was a real character who smoked 60 cigarettes a day, liked a drink and also loved gambling. He had a bet on the horses most days, and his best friend was Greville Starkey, a top-class jockey during the 1960s and 1970s.

We were playing in the reserves at West Brom and 'Taffy', as he was known, already had a copy of the *Sporting Life* spread out when I arrived at the Victoria Ground for departure to West Brom. I also like a bet so he had a fellow punter to converse with. He sat me down and told me that he had a 'certainty' to back on that Saturday. The horse's odds were 5/1 and I immediately rushed around to the betting shop, promptly putting a 'fiver' on the nose. At the time, my wages were £30.00 per week. Taffy was concerned about one thing only, the race was timed for 3.00 p.m. and the game kicked off at 3.00, by strange coincidence. West Brom were the only team in the country who had a TV in each dressing room.

On the way to the Hawthorns, Taffy's mind was working overtime. I know he had a right few quid on this horse, and he wanted to know the result a.s.a.p.

At ten minutes to kick-off, we went out on the pitch to warm up. When then official came out at three minutes to 3.00, Taffy went down with an injury. We started the game with ten men. At five minutes past 3.00, Taffy appeared on the touchline, and the referee gave the nod for him to reappear. He ran past me giving me a huge grin.

'T.C,' he said. 'It skated in at 5/1.'

An Argentinian international fly half who has won 26 caps:
he has scored 178 points and is the fourth highest points
scorer in the history of Argentinian rugby.

We were on the Argentina tour to Scotland in 1999 and, as is often the case during tours, there was time for a little rest and relaxation, golf being the players' choice.

In Scotland golf was a must, with so many fine courses across the country. We all arrived at a club and had been given a fantastic reception by the members, many of whom had turned up to watch us all tee off on their beloved 18 holes.

The 1st tee was slap-bang, straight in front of the clubhouse. There was quite a crowd of members who had wandered out to see the supposedly much-vaunted sportsmen tee off.

It was 'fourballs'. The first of us took up position, and cracked it down the middle. Looking nonchalant, he strode off the tee. Up stepped the second golfer, and with a fluent swing – put his ball in an A1 position. The crowd clapped at what was to them, a fine display by such talented individuals.

The third of the four Argentinian players wandered up, placed his ball on the tee and belted it into the distance. The members again erupted. 'What a sight,' they thought, seeing these international rugby players so able to turn their hand to golf and so masterful from the off.

The fly half, Josè Cilley, was the fourth player. He addressed the ball, swung back, then forth, failing in only one part of the swing – he missed the ball. He coughed nervously, trying to pretend that it was just a practice swing. The members, though, had gone silent. Swing number two, quicker this time as the nerves took hold. Swssssshhhh. Thin air. The ball stubbornly remained unmoved on the tee. There were now some embarrassed murmurs from the audience. Immediately he re-swung – CONTACT. As he looked into the distance he realised his ambitions were a little lofty. The ball had dribbled 20 yards, just past the ladies' tee.

The crowd was now totally divided – the players, who were desperately trying not to explode into hysterics, and the members who clearly felt duped by the first three players.

Cilley is a tenacious individual, so he immediately strode towards the ball to have another crack at it, dying to get away from the clubhouse as soon as possible.

SWISH … The ball didn't move. The club meanwhile disappeared from his hands and skyrocketed into the air, only to land … in a tree. The members were in shock, the players had now collapsed into uncontrollable laughter. What did he do? Up he went, into the tree, to take shot number five…

The moral of the story? Golf doesn't need to be good to be entertaining ….

ED COODE

The World Rowing champion in the Coxless Fours in 1999 and 2001; he finished just outside the medals in the 2000 Olympics, coming fourth with Greg Serle in the Coxless Pairs.

This tale involves a not-to-be-named rower in the British squad who, on his first international appearance, was a bit too nervous. Aware that he had to focus hard on the job at hand, he remained totally undistracted by all the other crews and officials throughout his warm-up. He then paddled confidently over to his stake boat and lined himself up straight down his lane. It was not until he had sat there for a few minutes that the rather disturbed starting umpire asked what he was doing, as he was facing 180 degrees in the wrong direction.

I only wish the umpire hadn't said anything and had just started the race.

DR STEPHANIE COOK

The 2000 Olympic Modern Pentathlon gold medal winner, she was also the European and World Modern Pentathlon champion in 2001.

On the morning of the women's modern pentathlon competition at the Olympic games in Sydney, Kate Allenby (Olympic bronze medallist) and I found ourselves having breakfast with Audley Harrison (Olympic gold medallist in boxing) at about 5 a.m. Audley had his gold medal fight later that afternoon and with a medal already guaranteed, he was in a jovial mood, tucking into a large fry-up. Kate and I still had a whole day of competition ahead of us and tentatively ate our muesli and bananas.

Later that day it was champagne all round as we celebrated our successes at the closing ceremony. Only one thing perplexed me, I couldn't quite work out why Audley had to get up at 5 a.m. when he was not fighting until the afternoon – I know I would have rather stayed in bed!

* * *

After winning the modern pentathlon World Championships in July 2001, I had a few days before I was due to resume my career as a doctor.

So in that time I travelled to Gujarat in India with Merlin (the British Charity that provides health care in crisis situations). An horrific earthquake devastated Gujarat in January 2001 and Merlin was working with the other relief organisations to help rebuild the primary care centres and provide hygiene and health care to those affected.

At one of the health care centres in the village of Ratnal where I was helping the local doctor with one of the clinics one day, there was a bit of a commotion outside – apparently word had got out that Steffi Graff – the great German tennis player was in town.

The locals were a little surprised at first when they saw me – I hardly have the shoulders of Steffi Graff – but were soon just as excited to be meeting an Olympic gold medallist instead!

SIR HENRY COOPER

A former two times British heavyweight Champion between 1959 and 1971, he fought Mohammed Ali twice, once famously knocking him to the canvas with 'Henry's Hammer'.

I was travelling up to Glasgow to play golf with the late Graham Hill, who was flying me up in his plane, which was plastered with adverts for a tobacco company and was nick-named 'the flying cigarette packet'.

Graham said to me, 'How high would you like me to fly the plane, Henry?'

I said, 'Three foot six inches – because that's my inside leg measurement and if necessary I can jump out.'

PETER CORMACK

A former Scotland international midfield footballer, he also played for Nottingham Forest and Liverpool and managed Partick Thistle and Hibernian.

The first time I met Bill Shankly, he asked me what I had been doing.

'Well Mr Shankly, I've just started pre-season training. I've been running through the woods and trees.'

'A' we'll son, that's for the birds.'

* * *

I was manager of Partick Thistle, and a very angry player came to see me.

'Come in, what's the problem?' I said.

The player's reply: 'Well, I'm not happy about my wages. What's this Nat-Ins?'

'Is this a wind-up?' I said. 'Everybody pays National Insurance.'

His retort: 'Well, I'm not too happy about it, but I'll pay it this week. But I'm not paying it next week.'

CHRIS COWDREY

A former international England cricketer who played 6 Test matches, he is perhaps most famous for captaining his country only once. It was during the 1988 Test series against the West Indies: he was injured and never captained England again. The right-handed batsman played his county cricket for Kent and Glamorgan.

One of the nicest cricketers ever to have played the game was Kent and England's Richard Ellison. He was extremely popular with both his own side and the opposition. Although he is actually quite intelligent, he was always a bit slow on the uptake, hence he rapidly earned the reputation for being a bit thick.

He was given the nickname 'Plank' by his Kent colleagues. After several months of answering to this name, he turned to us and said, 'Why am I called Plank?'

The reply from Kent player Graham Johnson was simply: 'Exactly, Richard.'

JOHN CRAWLEY

———————— •◆• ————————

An England cricketer with 33 Test caps to date, he made his Test debut v South Africa at Lord's in the 1st Test in 1994. He has scored 1,612 runs at an average of 34.29, and has a highest Test score of 156 not out – made against Sri Lanka in 1998. He is a former captain of Lancashire and plays for Hampshire, having scored 17,552 first class runs.

Bob Smith, my assistant programmer, can always be found hard at work at his desk. He works independently, without wasting company time talking to colleagues. Bob never thinks twice about assisting fellow employees, and always finishes given assignments on time. Often he takes extended measures to complete his work, sometimes skipping coffee breaks. Bob is a dedicated individual who has absolutely no vanity in spite of his high accomplishments and profound knowledge in his field. I firmly believe that Bob can be classed as an asset employee, the type that cannot be dispensed with. Consequently, I duly recommend that Bob be promoted to executive management, and a proposal will be executed as soon as possible.

Addendum: That idiot was standing over my shoulder while I wrote the report sent to you earlier today. Kindly re-read only the odd numbered lines.

D

LAWRENCE DALLAGLIO

*An England rugby union international who has won 48
caps to date. He has captained his country 14 times and was
a Lions tourist in 1997 and 2001.*

I was making my debut for Wasps against Harlequins, and as
ever in the clash between the two London clubs, it was a no-
holds-barred, full-on encounter. Both sides were giving it 120
per cent when there was an almighty ruck. Boots were flying
everywhere. It was a truly full-blooded confrontation.
Eventually the referee blew his whistle, and everyone clambered off the floor to reveal the man at the bottom of the pile
of bodies.

It was Will Carling.

He had a huge gash just under his eye. The referee – slightly
shaken that the England captain had been given such treatment in a match that he was refereeing, silenced everyone.

'Right,' he barked, 'own up, who did this?'

Immediately Carling's team-mate, Richard Langhorne, piped
up, 'Take your pick ref, it could have been one of 29 of us.'

* * *

I had been handed the captaincy of England, a huge honour and a role that I was very much looking forward to fulfilling. I was taking over from Phil de Glanville, he wished me the best of luck and ushered me aside: 'Just a little advice, as tradition goes from one outgoing skipper to the new one, take these.'

He handed me three white envelopes.

'If you fail to lead your team to victory, ' he said, 'open an envelope, and inside will be some invaluable advice as to how to proceed.'

The first match soon arrived – Australia in our own back-yard, a tough battle – two sides in transition with new players in both sides. The result? A 15–15 draw. My first match at the helm and we had failed to record a victory.

Immediately after the match I went to my bag and opened the first white envelope. 'Blame the referee,' it said.

I trotted into the press conference armed and ready.

'Well, it was a tight match, where small mistakes can change the complexion of the outcome, though I did feel that we weren't looked upon too kindly in some crucial decisions by the referee, and so we only managed a draw.'

The press swallowed that one. Phil de Glanville's envelope advice was already working a treat.

Match two – against the mighty All Blacks. A huge task for any side, and we had to be on the top of our game to beat arguably the best side in the world. We played up at Old Trafford to spread the rugby gospel and unfortunately we lost. Bad news, I would have to use the second of the three envelopes.

'Blame the kicker,' it said. Off I went to the press conference.

'Well, I felt that it was nip and tuck, we had the All Blacks under pressure and they were forced to give away penalties, but unfortunately Mike Catt didn't have the best of days with the boot and so the opportunities slipped away.'

The press seemed satisfied with that one – thank heavens for

70

these get-out-of-jail-free envelopes. I had, though, still failed as skipper to lead England to victory – bad news.

The third international was again against New Zealand. This time, though, it was back at the home of rugby – Twickenham. We were still progressing as a team and things were looking up. Still, the pressure was mounting on the players and most pertinently, on ME.

It turned out to be a classic. We raced into the lead – three cracking tries for England as we tore into the All Blacks. They clawed their way back, little by little, and – heartbreakingly – they managed to draw the match. I was gutted not to have won. I walked to the changing-room, looking forward to some first-class advice from the third and last white envelope. I rummaged in my bag, pulled it out and tore it open. The advice was simple: 'Start writing out three new envelopes.'

IAN DARKE

A radio and television broadcaster for the past 20 years, covering a series of Olympic Games and football World Cups. He is best known as a Sky Sports boxing commentator and has been at ringside for all the big fights involving top names like Lennox Lewis, Mike Tyson, Sugar Ray Leonard, Marvin Hagler and Prince Naseem Hamed.

Sebastian Coe, the great Olympic 1500 metre champion, goes as a VIP invited guest to support his favourite team, Chelsea, at Oxford United – only to be confronted by a bolshy old gateman who sees his Chelsea scarf and blocks his way into the posher part of the ground.

'Hey ... You're not comin' in here, mate...sod off with the other Chelsea hooligans down the other end,' says the gateman.

Seb tries to be polite and says reasonably that he is a special guest of the club.

'Not in here, you're not, mate. Go on, get down with all that other Chelsea rabbble.'

Eventually, getting a little exasperated, the great athlete says, 'But I am Sebastian Coe.'

'Won't take you long to get there then, will it?' said the gateman.

* * *

Interviewing Nigel Benn after he had won in 16 seconds (including the count) I asked for his reaction to the win. He said, 'Relieved, because I was well behind on points until I knocked him out.'

* * *

Commentating on a football match one day, I came out with the line for some reason: 'Justin Fashanu pounced on that chance like a black Frank Bruno.'

Of course, there is the football commentary of a Newcastle–Liverpool game when I said, 'This keeper, Hooper, ought to know his angles, he's got a degree in Maths ... or is it English Literature, I can't remember.'

" In my book, Dalrymple, that constitutes sledging. "

Kevin Darley is one of the few top current English jockeys
in a sport which is somewhat dominated by Irish riders.
He served his apprenticeship with Reg Hollinshead and rode
his first winner, Dust Up, at Haydock on his 17th birthday.
That proved to be the first of many victories as he was
crowned champion jockey in 2000, having ridden
155 winners.

Having worked in racing for many years now, you would hardly be surprised that the general topic of conversation when confronted by the racegoer is usually: 'Any tips for today, Kev?'

Finding it hard to resist, my reply is always: 'Never wash your hair with your hat on!'

You would be amazed at how many people ask, 'What time is the race that it's in?'

* * *

About five or six years ago The Jockey Club seemed to go through a spell of suspending jockeys for virtually anything. Whether it was the whip rule or causing interference to another horse, the headline in the racing daily *The Racing Post* generally started with another jockey being suspended.

At this time my youngest daughter, Gemma, aged seven or eight at the time, was just starting to take an interest in why Daddy was riding out at the crack of dawn and away at the races all the time. She used to browse through the *The Racing Post* to see where I was riding, etc. and obviously noticed all these suspensions being dished out.

Although falling foul of the rules on a couple of occasions during that season, this particular day was a genuine day off and for a pleasant change I decided to do the school run. After only a couple minutes into our journey, Gemma asked, 'Daddy, are you suspended?'

I replied, 'No, why?'

She then said, 'Then why are you taking us to school?'

To that, I had no answer.

DICKIE DAVIES

I was playing cricket for the 'Lord's Taverners' and my wife needed to get in touch. She rang the pavilion and asked to speak to Dickie Davies. She was told I'd just gone in to bat.

'That's all right,' she said, 'I'll hang on.'

* * *

Bill McLaren, the doyen of rugby commentators, had a rush of blood some years ago, and came out strongly with the words: 'Scotland for the World Cup – Scotland for the World Cup.'

It was diagnosed as a nasty case of premature 'E-jock-ulation'.

PHIL DE GLANVILLE

On arriving in Durban, South Africa, for the World Cup in 1995, we went out for our first training session on a pitch by the beach. We had been told to prepare for the thin air we would face when playing on the high veld of Pretoria and how hard it would be to breathe. Half-way through the session at Durban (half a mile from the sea!) Victor Ubogu was blowing hard at the pace set in the session, and as he got his breath back, was heard to say:

'Christ, this altitude is killing me!'

* * *

Playing golf one day, I walked past Nigel Redman desperately trying to hack a ball out of a bunker. I stopped and offered some advice: 'Nigel, why are you trying to use a four iron to hit that ball out of the bunker?' I asked.

Nigel replied, 'It wasn't a bloody bunker when I started.'

FRANKIE DETTORI

He rode every winner on a seven-race card at Ascot on 28 September 1996 and won the Prix de l'Arc de Triomphe twice and the Oaks three times. He has also won the 1000 & 2000 Guineas, the St Leger, the King George VI and Queen Elizabeth Diamond Stakes.

The first time I rode for the Queen at Royal Ascot, Lord Caernarvon (who was at the time the Queen's racing manager) came to the weighing room and asked if I had ever ridden for the Queen before.

I said 'no' and was told what to do when meeting her: 'Walk out into the paddock, call her "Your Majesty" first and then "Ma'am" after that.'

I practised in front of the mirror, touching my cap and so on. When the race came I rode the horse, came second – everyone was pleased. I jumped off and went to the weighing-room, no problems.

Then on Saturday I was riding for the Queen again, only this time there was no Lord Caernarvon. I went into the paddock, talking to another jockey and suddenly looked up to see the Queen standing there.

My mind went blank.

'Ow are you?' was all I could come up with.

'Still here Frankie,' she replied.

TED DEXTER

A former England international cricketer between 1958 and 1968, he scored 4,502 runs, had a Test average of 47 and scored 4,502 runs. His highest Test score was 205 against Pakistan in the 1961–62 series in Karachi, and took 66 Test wickets. Nicknamed 'Lord Ted', Dexter captained his country and Middlesex. He hit over 21,000 first class runs at an average of over 40. Dexter later became the England Chairman of Selectors.

You may have paid your Income Tax,
And bought your wife a hat;
Adjusted each domestic bill;
Reduced anxiety to nil.
Quite likely, too, you've made your will;
But – have you oiled your bat?

Perchance on questions ponderous,
In conference you've sat;
Mayhap you've met a potentate,
And settled grave affairs of state
That call for tact cannot wait;
But – have you oiled your bat?

Your conscience may be crystal-clear
On togs and things like that;
You may be waiting – unafraid
To turn out, spotlessly arrayed,
Complete with blazer (newly made)
But – HAVE YOU OILED YOUR BAT?

FAJ GODFREY (ancient)

* * *

There was an old man of Bengal,
Who purchased a bat and a ball,
Some gloves and some pads -
It was one of his fads -
For he never played cricket at all.

ALFRED AINGER (ancient)

TONY DIPROSE

*An England rugby union international who has captained
his country, he was a Lions tourist in 1997.*

We're at an England team meeting in Marlow before England v
Wales in 1997. It was a tactics session taken by head coach Jack
Rowell. Jack was using an overhead projector (OHP) to show
moves on a big screen.

Half-way through the meeting, to the players' amusement, a
fly landed on the OHP, producing a distorted image on the
screen among the scrums and line-outs.

To further laughter Jack Rowell then tried to get rid of the
image on the big screen itself. Obviously now confused, Jack,
the players now with tears in their eyes, goes round the back of
the screen to look for the offending fly, who was still crawling

on the OHP. Jack has totally lost his composure by now, the other management are in hysterics, and the episode was finally rounded off with Mark 'Ronnie' Regan shouting, 'You're village,' from the back of the room. He then hid!

DAMIAN D'OLIVEIRA

————— •◆• —————

A player and coach at Worcestershire CCC since 1982. He has a full set of winner's medals in domestic cricket, scoring 10 hundreds in his 9,476 first-class runs with a best of 237 v Oxford University in 1991.

While Ian Botham was at Worcestershire, I was in a bit of a bad nick (form) so I decided to ask the great man to have a look at my batting. After he had been watching me in the nets for 20 minutes, I asked what he thought. He said: 'Cut five inches off the bottom of your bat.'

'Do you think my bat is too big for me?'

He just turned away and said, 'No, but it will fit into the bin much easier.'

* * *

Sir Don Bradman and Dean Jones were playing a round of golf. On the 18th, it was all square. The 18th was a dog-leg right with some tall pine trees on the corner. Dean Jones had the honour and could not decide whether or not to try to go over the trees to cut the corner. He turned to Sir Don and said, 'When you were my age did you go over the trees?'

Sir Don without hesitation said, 'Yes.'

Dean Jones took on the trees but unfortunately caught the top of the branches and landed in the middle of the trees. Sir Don laid up to the middle of the fairway and had a perfect approach to the green.

As they walked to their balls, Dean Jones turned to Sir Don and said, 'We have better clubs now. Balls go farther and I could not have hit that any better, yet you used to clear the trees and I couldn't.'

Sir Don walked on calmly and said, 'When I was your age, these trees were only three feet tall.'

WADE DOOLEY

A former England rugby union international who won 55 caps. He was a World Cup finalist in 1991 and won the Grand Slam in 1991 and 1992. The 6'8" second row was a Lions tourist in 1989.

It was 30 March, 1985, Ireland v England at Lansdowne Road – my first encounter with the Irish. There was a line-out to Ireland on the half-way line, 20 minutes into the game and we were really struggling to crack the Irish coded system.

Line-outs in those days were free-for-alls, and the calls were getting more and more complicated to confuse the opposition and secure your own line-out ball. The Irish hooker held the ball high and gave the command: 'Green, Limerick, Guinness. Beatles, Peter O'Toole, 2916.'

As we hastily pondered the various permutations and possibilities, with the hooker about to unleash the ball, a voice rang out from the Irish second row line-out jumper Donal Lenihan: 'BLOODY HELL, ME AGAIN!'

* * *

After England's Grand Slam victory against France at Twickenham in 1991, amid the post-match changing-room disarray and celebrations, the mighty Mick 'The Munch' Skinner decides to take an early bath so that he can get on the beer undisturbed. The changing room door opens and the then Prime Minister John Major (a keen rugby follower) is escorted in by the President of the RFU to congratulate the victorious England team.

The first person they meet is a very naked Mick Skinner emerging from the bath/shower area, busily drying himself off with towel in his left hand while attending to his vanity, jiggling his lunchbox/meat and two veg with his right hand.

John Major is confronted by Mick who holds out his right hand and greets the PM with the welcome: 'Yo John!! Top man, large, bosh, put it there, how's it hanging?' (Mick always talks in Geordie code like that.)

To the horror of the RFU President and the amusement of the England players – and all credit to the Prime Minister who must have momentarily considered a quick exit – John Major took the hand that had seconds earlier been in contact with Mick Skinner's lunchbox and retorted, 'Obviously not as well as you, Mr Skinner.'

* * *

The Irish rugby union team are on tour in Japan and asleep in the team hotel when there is a massive earthquake that destroys all the buildings.

Searching the rubble were the Japanese search and rescue teams with their sniffer dogs and listening devices. They hear a faint voice from under the rubble of the hotel: 'It's Keith Wood, the Irish captain. Is anyone there?'

'Keith! Is that you? Are you all right? Keep talking. Where are you? We are going to get you out.'

'Yes it's me, I can hear you. I'm OK. I am in room 303.'

*A commentator on the BBC's Test Match Special in the
1960s and 1970s and a broadcaster on three Olympic
Games for ITV, he was also a successful television and radio
producer. Neil played cricket and hockey for the Combined
Services and is a former Chairman of the Lord's Taverners.
He also formulated the blueprint in the 1980s for the rugby
World Cup and is a patron of the Motor Neurone Disease
Association.*

My first-ever broadcast was a live three-minute cricket report
for a BBC Radio Sports programme. I spent the whole day
taking copious notes on the match I was covering and duly
arrived at Broadcasting House by taxi at about 7.00 p.m. for
the broadcast at 7.30. When I walked into the control room
the producer immediately saw the state of rising panic I was in,
with just half an hour to go, so he asked me if he could give
me any advice.

'Please, anything,' I mumbled.

'Sit in that corner over there and learn the first sentence of
your report off by heart. You will find the nerves will start to go
and you'll begin to feel more confident.'

I took his advice and said to myself over and over again in
the corner, 'I've just come back from the Oval where Surrey are
playing Yorkshire … I've just come back from the Oval …'. I got
it off pat.

At 7.29 I took my place in the studio opposite the presenter
of the programme and at 7.30 precisely the red light went on.
To my absolute horror his opening words were, 'This is the
BBC Home Service and I'm going to hand you straight over to
Neil Durden-Smith who has just come back from the Oval
where Surrey are playing Yorkshire.'

So, when I could get them out, my first words to the great

British Public were, 'As the announcer has just told you , I've just returned from th Oval where Surrey are playing Yorkshire!'

My second broadcast was much easier.

* * *

The occasion was the historic match between Ireland and the West Indies at Sion Mills which I was covering for BBC Television on 2 July, 1969.

I travelled in the same car from the hotel to the ground as Clyde Walcott (the manager), Lance Gibbs and Basil Butcher, captain of the touring side for the day. On the way Butch asked what he should do if he won the toss.

'Bat', I said, 'because if you field first and bowl Ireland out before lunch you will disappoint the huge crowd they are expecting, and the television audience too.'

He duly won the toss and batted. The rest is history. The West Indies were bowled out for 25 and Ireland won by nine wickets. I've never been allowed to forget it!

DAVID DUCKHAM

An England rugby union international, he earned 36 caps between 1969 and 1976. Famed for his sidestep, he was a Lions tourist to New Zealand in 1971. Such were his perfor-mances on that tour, including a record six tries in a mid-week game, that many Welsh fans referred to 'Dai' Duckham as an honorary Welshman!

This is a true story.

The records will show that in April 1973 I captained Coventry Rugby Football Club to victory against Bristol at Twickenham in the final of rugby's equivalent of the FA Cup, known as the (then unsponsored) Rugby Football Union (RFU) Knockout Cup Competition.

At some point early in the first half of the final, the Bristol (and England) captain John Pullin was forced to leave the field with a badly gashed lower leg. He wasn't fit to resume and so his team were down to 14 players for the rest of the game because there were no substitutes allowed in those days.

Despite this handicap, Bristol then proceeded to play like men possessed and very nearly got control of the game. However, they ran out of steam later on and Coventry eventually achieved a fairly comfortable victory – I can't remember the final score!

At an after-match press interview I must have admitted to being in some way embarrassed by the way that our opponents had fought back strongly for much of the match after John Pullin's departure and had nearly got on top.

Four days later, someone sent me a press cutting from the *Yorkshire Evening Post*, which was a report of the match. It included a picture of me, along with the headline: 'Duckham Embarrassed'.

The anonymous sender had attached his own note to this cutting, with the words: 'Having read the attached report, I can understand your embarrassment!'

The first paragraph read as follows: 'Coventry captain David Duckham admitted to being embarrassed after leading his side to victory in the Final of the RFU Kockout [!!!] Cup Competition.'

E

MALCOLM EDMUNDS

——◆——

A former Cornwall county golf champion and Royal Navy golf champion.

Many years ago I played a practice round at Royal Cinque Ports Golf Club with a fellow competitor. It was the first time either of us had played the course and I happened to remark to him about the cavernous bunkers and the greens which were like putting on velvet.

After our round we were having a drink in the bar when my fellow competitor was engaged in conversation by an elderly ex-Royal Marine general who was a member. The ex-general asked if he had enjoyed the course to which he replied: 'The greens were pure velvet and brilliant.'

This pleased the ex-general who then asked if there was anything about the course that he disliked?

To which he replied, 'The *carnivorous* bunkers.'

A former England international cricketer who played 80 Test matches for England, scoring 12 centuries, seven of which were against Australia. His highest score was 310 not out against New Zealand in 1965 at Headingley. He also captained Surrey for five years, hitting 103 centuries in his first-class career.

During my cricket and business career I have done much travelling around the world and below I have highlighted some notices I have seen in various establishments:

In a Hong Kong dentist's reception: 'TEETH EXTRACTED BY THE LATEST METHODISTS.'

In a laundry in Rome: 'LADIES LEAVE YOUR CLOTHES HERE AND SPEND THE AFTERNOON HAVING A GOOD TIME.'

In the window of a Swedish furrier: 'FUR COATS MADE FOR LADIES FROM THEIR OWN SKIN.'

In a Copenhagen airline ticket office: 'WE TAKE YOUR BAGS AND SEND THEM IN ALL DIRECTIONS.'

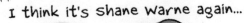

Turn my googly, you crazy sheila!
Go on, twist my flipper...

JONATHAN EDWARDS

*Having won silver at the 1996 Olympics, he went one better
at Sydney in 2000, winning the gold in dramatic
circumstances. He also has World Championship and
Commonwealth gold medals in his full collection.*

In the World Championships in Seville in 1999, I performed
particularly badly. It transpired that it was a problem with my
run-up and the fact that it was too short.

How could that be? Well, I used to measure my approach in
foot lengths and didn't realize that when I changed sponsors at
the start of that season my new shoes were 1 cm shorter. As a
result, my run-up was nearly one and a half metres shorter
than normal. I've heard of a bad workman blaming his tools,
but I guess this takes it to a new level!

* * *

Apparently thieves recently broke into the Stadium of Light,
and hearing the news, Peter Reid rushed to the ground.

'Did they get the cups?' he asked.

'No, sir,' came the reply. 'They didn't reach the canteen!'

TRACY EDWARDS

*Round-the-world sailor who made history in 1990 by
captaining the first all-female crew in the Whitbread Round
The World Race on Maiden.*

When joining my first 'proper' racing maxi yacht in Cape
Town, I had to persuade a sceptical and less than enthusiastic
male crew that I could manage the job. The boat was *Atlantic*

Privateer and we were competing in the 1985–86 Whitbread round the world yacht race.

The start was delayed by 30 minutes and all the yachts were wondering why. A coastguard boat came out to us and everyone then found out why the entire fleet had been delayed.

I had forgotten my passport and they had brought it out to me!

* * *

While attempting the Jules Verne record, for non-stop circumnavigation of the world, we were racing our 92 ft catamaran through the treacherous wastes of the Southern Ocean.

Miki van Koskull, one of my watch captains, came on deck ready for her watch and was wearing her survival suit for the first time. She was complaining that it was very uncomfortable. After a while one of the girls saw something; Miki had the clothes hanger still inside …

JOHN EMBUREY

An England cricketer between 1978 and 1995, he scored over 1,700 runs and took 147 wickets. He is the current Middlesex coach.

Back in 1995, Middlesex were playing Glamorgan at Lord's. I was bowling and it was turning out to be a very lucrative day for Middlesex, we were on form and I was happily managing to rattle through their batting line-up.

First up, I got Hugh Morris, all 5′8″ of him, lbw – off he trudged. Then in came Tony Cottee, who was one of the smallest players I had ever played against – only 5′3″. He soon departed to the pavilion. Next in strode Adrian Dalton, who stood no taller than 5′7″ in his socks. We were having a bit of a giggle at this point at the vertically challenged batting line-up. Dalton was quick to depart too – caught Roseberry, bowled Emburey. As he wandered back to the pavilion I said, 'Well lads, that's three of the seven dwarves out, I wonder who we are going to get next, Snow White?'

Who walked in? Otis Gibson. The 6'4" West Indian fast bowler – wrong call Embers!

FAROKH ENGINEER

A former Indian international cricketer who played 46 Test matches between 1962 and 1976. He once scored the fastest ever century for India against the West Indies. He played county cricket for Lancashire and is now a broadcaster.

I was playing a round of golf with Bobby Charlton at our local course – 'Mere Golf & Country Club' – and as I was lining up this rather crucial putt, Bobby suddenly asked me, 'Are you aware of the war that is going on at the moment between Pakistan and your country of birth, India?'

'Of course I am,' came my reply.

A few seconds later as I was ready, settled and about to putt, Bobby once again interrupted and asked me jokingly, 'Will you be going out there to fight for India?'

'Yes,' I replied, 'but only if the fighting gets nearer to my village.'

'What is your village actually called?'

'Oswaldtwistle, right in the heart of Lancashire, so I think I'm alright for the moment!'

* * *

Just as I was about to tee off at the Kiawah Island golf course in South Carolina, I was suddenly approached by a stranger who introduced himself as 'Kev'.

'Could I join you? he asked politely.

'Of course,' I replied. I was on my own so it would be nice to have some company. I introduced myself by my first name, 'Farokh.'

'Kev,' came the reply.

I thoroughly enjoyed his company although he seemed a bit of a nutter, the most annoying aspect being that he kept on calling me 'Frank', in spite of my repeatedly reminding him it was actually 'Farokh'. No good, still he kept on calling me Frank.

When we eventually finished, 'even' after a wonderful day, we adjourned to the bar at the 19th. After a quick drink Kev suggested, 'Why don't we meet again later at the Kiawah Inn for a meal or something?'

Later that night he approached me and my wife on the lawns shouting, 'Hi Frank.'

I introduced him. 'This is Kev,' I said.

Julie, my wife, turned to me: 'Do you know *his* correct name? You only introduced him as "Kev".'

A few moments later Julie went direct to the man himself: "You wouldn't be *the* Kevin, Kevin Costner would you?'

He was delighted. At last someone recognised him.

In my defence, this was around 1991 when he was virtually unknown. He still calls me 'Frank' every time he calls or emails and on his Christmas cards, but somehow I have found it in my heart to forgive him!

F

NICK FALDO

*Europe's greatest ever golfer with over 42 titles to his credit,
he is a six-times Major winner. He won the Open on three
occasions, in 1987, 1990 and 1992 and the Masters in
1989, 1990 and 1996. In 1977, aged 20, he became the
youngest-ever Ryder Cup team member and proceeded to
win all his matches, including victories over Tom Watson
and Jack Nicklaus. He represented Europe a record 11 times
and to this day holds the record for the number of points
and matches won in the competition.*

I was practising one day when someone came up and asked if
they could stand and watch me. I hit four perfect balls and I
then stood back and took a practice swing, which is when my
so-called fan turned round and said:

'Did you know that your practice swing is not the same as
your actual swing?'

I packed up my clubs and went home.

ANDREW FARRELL

*The Wigan and Great Britain rugby league captain has 11
caps for England and 23 caps for Great Britain, and has
over 2,800 career points. Farrell has won the Challenge Cup
with Wigan in 1993, 1994, 1995 and 2002, and
captained the club to its first-ever Grand Final win in 1998.*

A few seasons ago, Wigan adopted a mascot and, being known
as the Pie Eaters, our mascot was a giant pie, an enormous roly-
poly pie. Our Great Britain centre Gary Connolly discovered that
the mascot's suit was left at the ground overnight. One morning
he decided to sneak in early, unbeknown to the coaching staff
and try the pie on. It fitted a treat and soon Gary was roaming
all over the training pitch suited and booted as a giant pie.

Unfortunately disaster was just around the corner. Weighed
down by the weight of the pie, Gary toppled over and ended
up flat on his back. He couldn't get back up and, needless to
say, none of the lads would give him a hand. Having been
early for training he ended being the only player late and
copped a fine. He hoped to get away with it, but those hopes
turned out to be … PIE in the sky.

JOHN FEAVER

*A former international tennis player, having represented
Great Britain in the Davis Cup between 1977 and 1980.
He was one of the biggest servers of his era and still plays
doubles in the Wimbledon seniors with John Lloyd. Feaver
is also the Championship Director at Eastbourne.*

I was playing in the third round of the 1980 British
Hardcourt Championships in Bournemouth. Everything was

going well, I was mentally prepared, physically warmed-up and ready for action.

As I entered the arena there were 2,500 fans keenly waiting to see my match with Angel Gimenez of Spain.

Relishing the atmosphere and keen to do well in front of my family and friends who were out in force, I took off my track-suit bottoms, only to discover …I had forgotten my shorts.

Red-faced and rueful after 2,500 pairs of eyes had clocked me in my jockstrap, I recovered my dignity and returned to the changing room to collect the missing item. I actually went on to match point, but it was one of those days all round – I lost.

CARL FOGARTY

Quite simply a legend of World Superbike Racing, the crowd worshipped his gutsy, aggressive style and determination that won him an incredible four World Superbike titles.
He retired in 2000 because of injury and is now the team owner of Foggy Petronas Racing.

The travelling side of racing is not as glamorous as everyone may think and the 30-hour journey back from Australia is always the worst. So it was always a blessing when you were finally picked up from the airport and on the final leg home – unless it was my Dad there to meet us!

In 1997, we were met by my Dad, only to be told that he couldn't remember where he had parked the car at Manchester Airport. After tramping round for what seemed like ages with our suitcases, we eventually found his Mitsubishi Shogun. Then he couldn't find the exit ticket that he'd paid for. He did, however, spot one on the floor and decided that this might work at the barrier, rather than having to fork out any more cash. Sure enough, after driving up to the machine, we were told that the ticket was invalid so Dad had to reverse out so that everyone else could get out.

Instead of seeking assistance he then came up with the bright idea of trying to follow one of the other drivers out before the barrier came down. He picked on a Mercedes owner to help out but the guy just looked at him like he was an idiot as Dad tried to gesture his plan. Even so, Dad was determined to give it a go. The only problem was that he only got into first gear as the Merecedes was long gone and the barrier half-way down. It caught the top of our car and broke off so that it was left hanging like a broken arm. My mate and fellow racer, Jamie Whitham, was crying with laughter – Dad didn't seem to find it as funny!

DUNCAN FORBES

————————◆————————

Duncan's professional career began at Colchester United in 1961 and he had played 270 times for the Layer Road side before Norwich signed him for £10,000 in September 1968. Duncan made 357 appearances in yellow and green, scoring 12 times, and was never sent off. Forbes won the English Second Division championship with Norwich in the 1971–72 season. He spent 33 years at Carrow Road: 13 as a player, seven on the commercial staff and then 13 as Chief Scout.

After we had got through to Wembley, we had an impromptu party at our bungalow. It was very crowded, and in the kitchen one of the players leaned back on our cooker and accidentally turned it on. His suit jacket caught alight and someone said, 'Never mind, it'll be a blazer now.'

Some believe the pool facilities cost Birmingham the Commonwealth Games.

Although not a natural ventriloquist, George found that if he moved his fingers the girls would make a noise.

Dennis found he could only watch television on his back with his
new glasses.

Foggy wasn't sure that he could win another championship on the new
Ducati, but he'd give it a go.

'… and he couldn't quite
get his leg over …'

Faldo couldn't see Fanny
for the bush.

The players had to take the batteries out of the new automated umpire to stop him stealing the jumpers.

Luckily Carling had kept the receipt for his aftershave.

Blown off his horse by a freak gust of wind, Frankie Dettori was grateful to the crowd who caught him.

The tabloid mudslingers were beginning to get to some of the England boys.

Willie takes delivery of his new
mobile phone, handmade in Lilliput.

'I know you're in there Gower!'

Dallaglio, in peak fitness for the World Staring Championships, found the
subbuteo team tough opponents.

Jimmy soon realised Riverdance was not what the crowd had come to see.

Some players found it hard to cope on tour without their partners.

'Oi! Have you seen my turnips!'

Mike Gatting was delighted to discover that he hadn't eaten all the pies after all.

Joke: When I was in Australia playing football, I was bitten by a kangaroo. It made me hopping mad.

Joke: What is the richest country in the world? Ireland, because its capital is always Dublin.

MARK FOSTER

A swimmer who holds the world record for the 50m freestyle and was the 50m Freestyle world champion in 1993, 1999 and 2000.

Q: Why did the American football team go to the phone booth?
A: To get their quarter back.

Q: Why aren't the England football team allowed to own a dog?
A: Because they can't hold on to a lead.

Q: What do you call bears with no ears?
A: B.

A man walks into a bar and says, 'Who the bloody hell put that there?'

*The winner of seven National Hunt championships in
a ten-year period, he rode 1,038 winners and is now
a TV broadcaster.*

When I first went for an interview as an apprentice at Fred
Winter's, he was concerned that I was too heavy to be a jockey.

'What is the lightest you have ever been?' he asked.

'About 7lb 3oz,' I replied.

He was not amused.

* * *

Years ago, when I was an apprentice, I was given a ride by a
trainer. It was the first time that I had been offered a ride and I
was keen to make a good impression. Well, the race came and
went in a flash. Unfortunately I finished last. When I got off I
saw the trainer striding up to me:

'Congratulations,' he said. 'You have just had two outings in
one go.'

'What do you mean?' I replied, innocently.

'That was your *first* ride for me, and your *last*.'

G

KIRSTY GALLACHER

A presenter on Sky Sport's 90 minutes *and Channel 4's*
Rise, *Kirsty is the daughter of the former Ryder Cup
captain, Bernard Gallacher.*

It was the first day of filming 'Nick Faldo's Junior Masterclass',
a video specifically targeted at getting youngsters to take up
golf. I was 15 and my golf was actually quite good, hence I had
been chosen out of many young hopefuls. We'd been practising all morning and finally it was time to start shooting the
video. Typically I was chosen to hit the first shot.

I stood on the first tee with Nick Faldo – the best golfer in
the world at the time – looking over me. I took the club back,
completely missed the ball and, as I was bringing the club back
down with one hand (terribly embarrassed) I hit the ball clean
into Nick's shin. I don't think I would have been that accurate
even if I'd tried ….

Faldo still has the scar to prove it – which he likes to remind
me of whenever I see him!

A former New Zealand rugby union international, he
played rugby league for Leeds and is now a Sky TV analyst.

I was on tour with the 1989 All Blacks tour to Wales, Ireland and Canada. We had come to Wales just after the Canada leg and always knew this part of the trip would be especially tough. The Welsh team were going through some tough times in the 1980s, but we knew that the club sides were a totally different kettle of fish – very strong, hugely competitive and with fantastic support as well.

We spent most of our time based in The Grand Hotel in Cardiff, as most of the club sides were accessible from there. One day early on the tour we were walking down the shopping mall, getting a breath of fresh air and there was this old gentleman sitting on a bench. He saw the silver fern on our clothes and said, 'Oh boys, who have you got tomorrow?'

'Cardiff,' we replied.

'Cardiff will beat you,' he said. 'Cardiff are a good side. They will beat you.'

We played Cardiff, had to battle hard, but we won. A few days later someone else would see him and he would ask, 'Oh boys, who are you playing next?'

'Newport,' came the reply.

'Newport, good side, tough side, Rodney Parade, wide ground, they will beat you.'

So, we beat Newport, albeit hard again.

We played them all. Neath, at the time, were the Welsh champions.

'Neath will beat you.'

Llanelli up at Stradey. 'Llanelli, at home, big crowd. They will beat you.' So the predictions went on. We came through all the club games unscathed.

It came to the Test match; it was the Friday before the Saturday game at Cardiff Arms – a full house expected and all to play for. The Welsh are obviously very proud, very passionate about their rugby and it was *the* fixture, especially for us Kiwis who were really looking forward to it. There I was with a couple of mates the day before the big match, walking down the street when we came across the old Welshman again.

'Oh hello boys, you are the All Blacks aren't you?'
'Yes that's right,' we replied.
'Who have you got tomorrow?'
'Wales.'
'Oh, Wales, they are bloody crap, you'll beat them!'

JASON GANNER

Ex-manager of the England badminton team and the trainer for the Barcelona Olympics in 1992, Ganner has coached and trained badminton players across the globe.

Upon arriving in Paris with my partner Peter Penekett, to play doubles in the French Open, we were shown to our accommodation. The Racing Club de Paris is a beautiful ornate building nestling in sight of the Eiffel Tower – a fantastic location.

Historically badminton players are not known for their luxurious lifestyles, often going to tournaments on a shoestring, even though representing your country. We thought it would be no different on this occasion and therefore we had taken our 'nosebags' full of all sorts of sustenance such as Vesta curries – you know the sort, a dried mass that showed no resemblance to a meal but, when cooked, tasted like nectar to a poor badminton player! Plus of course the camping gas stove, our most treasured possession.

Upon arrival, we were shown to our room three storeys up in an attic room at the front of the club – not quite what we anticipated in this luxurious abode, but we were grateful all the same as it was 8 p.m. on a Friday. We were tired from the journey and knew that we were due to play early Saturday morning, so we needed to eat and get some sleep. We decided to cook our curry; Peter went off down the corridor to fill our billycan with water (no *en suite* here) and proceeded to cook the chicken curry.

This done, I was given the billycan to dispose of the remaining starchy sludge that closely resembled rice. This posed a problem as there was no sink or loo to pour it down, the bathroom was at the end of the corridor the next floor down and we were already regretting the curry smell as it was breaking the house rules, so I decided to throw the contents out of the little window into the gutter. As you can imagine we were really chuffed with our circumstances, a posh hotel (except our room) a full stomach and the promise of a quick stroll before bedtime, so after unpacking and preparing our kit and rackets for the next day we ventured out.

Half-way down the stairs we heard an almighty commotion from below. As we got closer we noticed people arriving at the club, ladies dressed in ball gowns and the gents in black ties. The noise got louder and louder until we arrived at the ornate grand entrance. We, of course, wondered what they were looking at and joined the melee, dressed in our shell suits, only to see a lava-like flow of rice particles and slippery sludge running down each step and onto the pavement. Then, almost in slow motion, everyone's eyes followed the flow, up the steps to the front wall of the building.

With a quick step backwards you could see this gunge spreading forth from the *broken* gutter just below our room window. The whole contents of the billycan had worked its way down the front of this building, weaved in and out of the carved architecture, down to the steps and out onto the pavement, where it seemed to have congealed onto the hems of ball gowns and the dainty shoes of the ladies!

Peter and I looked at each other, both of our jaws hitting the ground. In one movement we both turned on our heels and power-walked in the opposite direction. Needless to say our quick night-time stroll in Paris turned into a very late night to avoid any confrontation!

As it turned out not a word was said about this to us, but Peter and I were never invited back again to take part in the tournament.

* * *

Back in the late 1960s my brother David and I were picked to play together for our club 'Treloars' for the first time. We were to play in the Alton Drill Hall, which at that time was used by the ATC and Territorial Army. In those days not so much care was taken over health and safety, and careful storage of items was unheard of.

The match started with David and myself playing first. We were used to good lighting in our hall but on this occasion the Drill Hall only had gas lighting. Mind you, in those days a hall with a roof intact was a luxury! We were only into the fourth rally of the match when I decided to hit a high defensive shot clear up towards our opponents' ceiling. What happened next was just incredible.

The shuttlecock continued its flight through the gas light and came out the other side a feathered fireball, downwards not towards the court – but towards the store for the thunder flashes. You've guessed it – the feathered fireball landed on top of one of the thunder flashes which immediately sparked the fuse, whereupon we all hit the deck. There was an almighty series of cracks and flashes followed by a huge cloud of dust. Once the dust settled, there was a long silence followed by hysterical laughter, all you could see were these white faces of the rest of the team appearing from behind the wooden horse and gym equipment where they had taken refuge, while we were rolling around in the dust on the badminton court, hurting with laughter.

Just a footnote, nobody was hurt, Treloars won the match, and the night truly got my career off to a BANG!

JOHN R GARNER

A golfer who financed his early career by selling shares in himself, he was a member of the Ryder Cup sides of 1971 and 1973.

1967. The Daks, Wentworth Golf Club – The Burma Road.

I was playing the third round and being a young pro I couldn't afford a caddy – cost 16/6d (new money 82 ½p). So I was waiting for my name to be called at the 1st tee. The starter came over and said, 'Are these your clubs, son?'

'Yes,' I replied, 'these are mine.' (Two in my set were hickory-shafted – a putter and a niblick that I could make talk.)

He said, 'Well, turn around and I'll put the caddy's bib on.'

I thought this a bit restrictive but being a north-country lad, didn't complain as I'd qualified along with big names like Peter Allis and Christy O'Connor and just wanted to do my best and play golf.

The bib was no. 49 with Garner, JR printed on it, front and back. I put my glove on, put four tees and a marker in my pocket and took a brand new Dunlop 65 for my round. The starter duly called my name over the tannoy system and I walked in front of a reasonable crowd to peg up my ball, feeling nervous about the occasion but not the bib. As you do, I had a practice swing, stepped up to the ball, took my stance and aimed the face down behind the ball towards the fairway. Just before I took the club back, the starter shouted out, 'Hey, what do you think you are doing?'

'I'm going to hit it,' I replied.

'I thought you were caddying!'

'I am,' I said, 'but I am also playing!!'

WARREN GATLAND

A former rugby union coach of Ireland and currently the Director of Rugby at Wasps.

I am a born and bred Kiwi and although I feel that my accent is more than understandable, there were times during my time as coach of Ireland that the boys, to their cost, got the wrong end of the stick. My Kiwi accent has sometimes caused slight problems, various words can get misconstrued, for instance…

In the lead up to the second Test in Australia, Peter Clohessy, the uncompromising Irish prop, was having trouble sleeping. He was a terrible insomniac, and had tried all ways of getting a good night's rest. Well, on the morning of the Test, I was keen to know that Clohessy, one of the men who was to bear the brunt of Australia's aggression and hand out a little of our own controlled fire, had had a good night's sleep. So I wandered up to him: 'Peter, how did you sleep?' I said.

'Oh, great,' he replied.

'Did you have a pill to relax yourself?' To which he looked slightly surprised that I should have asked specifically how he got his fine night's kip, but chuckled: 'Yeh, yeh I did,' with a broad grin on his face.

'Did you get one off the Doc?'

'What?' he replied, looking slightly indignant this time.

'Did you get a sleeping pill off the Doc?'

'Aw, fook, is that what you meant, I tought you'd asked me if Io'd had a pull, not a pill!'

* * *

Trevor Brennan, one of our fine back row players, was feeling a bit tired at training and wandered up to me to ask if I had any suggestions.

'Well, perhaps four to five bananas at training.'

Anyway, next day he walks over a little gingerly, looking slightly embarrassed. 'Gats,' he said, 'I've tried, but today I've only managed 29.'

'No,' I said. 'Four TO five, not FORTY FIVE!'

" WE'RE POTHOLERS "

CALUM GILES

*Former England international hockey player, scoring
111 goals in 143 internationals.*

It was after we had just beaten the Germans, who were
favourites to win the 1995 European Cup in Dublin, my first
major. I was at the table and leaned back in my chair, trying to
give the impression of confidence and being laid back. I was
asked my first question.

'How does it feel having just beaten the Germans who are
favourites and having scored two of the goals as well?'

My reply: 'Well, obviously it's great, you always dream of ...',
when suddenly the majority of the room shouted out, 'SPEAK
UP!'

So I sat up and began again, 'Well obviously it's great, you
always dream of beating ...'.

Again a shouted interruption: 'USE THE MICROPHONE!'

So I dragged a microphone over and began again, 'Well
obviously it's great, you always dream of ...'.

Another shouted interruption: 'TURN THE THING ON!'

So I did, I composed myself and after a pause and in a strong
confident voice said, 'I'm very sorry, I've forgotten the question.'

NICK GILLINGHAM

*Winner of three consecutive European swimming titles,
a Commonwealth and World gold medal winner, and an
Olympic silver and bronze medallist during a six-year run
from 1988 to 1994.*

I recently went swimming with my five-year-old son. On this
particular day the water seemed particularly cold. Half-way

through our fun swim session we went for a nature break. Needless to say, when standing in the Gents, my son made the statement, 'Your willie has lost weight!'

I took a warm shower before returning home ….

GRAHAM GOOCH

A former England international cricketer who scored 8,900 Test runs at an average of 42 between 1975 and 1995. He captained his country and hit 333 against India in 1990 at Lord's.

Jack van Geloven, a pleasant, if rather strict northerner who used to play for Leicester, later became an umpire. At Tunbridge Wells once, against Kent, the last ball before lunch, Ray East is caught at mid-wicket, the fielder diving forward, just scooping the ball up. Ray thinks it's a bump-ball so he just stands there. Van Geloven has a little think and then, up comes his finger: 'Out.'

On the way in for lunch, Ray walks in with Jack, saying, 'Okay, I'm off, Jack, but I could swear it was a bump-ball.'

'Get away, lad, that was a fair catch, you're out.'

All through lunch, as we're all sitting there, Ray is still rucking on that he wasn't out and it was a bump-ball. Jack sits there having his tuck and thinking quietly, 'I dunno, what's the world coming to? East was out and that's all there is to it.'

So the bell goes. Out go the umpires, out go the Kent players. East is in the dressing room, putting on a different coloured helmet, different gloves and bat. And out he goes again. Van Geloven had no idea, of course. Ray is at Jack's end, and just as the bowler is about to deliver the first ball after lunch, East turns his new helmet to Van Geloven, looks him straight in the eye, and says, 'You did say that was a bump-ball, didn't you, Jack?'

Van Geloven leapt out of his skin and nearly collapsed on the spot.

People like Van Geloven, the veterans who have seen it all and done it all as players are like old and firm friends, sort of uncles in charge on the beach. Remember old Arthur Jepson of Nottinghamshire? Dusty Miller came in to bat once.

'Mornin', Arthur.'

'Mornin',Dusty lad. Did you use the motorway this morning …?' or 'Ee lad, I've a gippy tummy after that breakfast she gave me,' that sort of general friendly chat. So this time, when Arthur says, 'You'll have no trouble on this pitch, Dusty lad, the others don't seem to realise it, but all you've got to do is get right forward every time and this bowling is a heap of crap.'

Right, thinks Miller, nice nod and a wink there from old Jeppo, thanks very much. So next over, Dusty is facing, and Arthur is at the bowler's end. First ball, he plays the most extravagant forward defensive of all time, right down the track with his long left leg. Just like Arthur had said. It hits him in the middle of the pad. Big appeal. Finger up.

'That's plumb, lad, sorry!' said Jepson, as he sent him on his way.

* * *

There are good umpires and bad everywhere in cricket. Some Pakistani umpires are good, some English umpires are not and vice versa. But if a cricketer is not prepared to take the rough with the smooth it would be anarchy and the cricket would be dead in no time. Without umpires there would be no game.

Whenever any question of umpiring comes up, I always try to tell myself – and especially if I think I might have been 'sawn off at the knees,' as we professionals put it, by a poor decision – is that they all love cricket. They wouldn't be doing the job if they didn't love cricket in the first place.

When I first came into the game in the 1970s, there were lots of umpires who had played the game in the 1950s: Arthur Jepson, Jack Crapp, Sam Cook, Dusty Rhodes. Lovely characters. As captain, you have a form to mark at the end of each match on the umpire's 'performance' and it goes back to Lord's. I nearly always just ticked the 'Good to Satisfactory' box. One really bad decision doesn't affect this but if, say, there were three real blunders from one umpire in a game, then I would mark him 'down' a bit. Once, the story goes, our captain 'Tonker Taylor' had marked down the old Aussie umpire and character, Cec Pepper, 'for over-excessive and noisy farting.'

Basically, the way to bracket umpires is in three types; a bowling umpire, a batting umpire, or a captain's umpire. The last one does make a bit of sense, seeing that the captain is marking up after the game, but I suppose it's a hark back to the old days of amateur captains when they could be very strict, even tyrannical, with 'working class' umpires. And sure, sometimes when you are given 'not out' in a very close lbw decision, you can say to yourself 'Yep, a good 'Captain's decision', that.'

A famous bowler's umpire was someone like Eddie Phillipson, the former Lancashire opening bowler, who would give lots of lbws, no fear, nor favour, nor favourites. If it hit the pad, up would go the finger. Once David Acfield had Eddie at his end, so naturally David was being a bit appeal-happy. Up goes another lbw shout. 'Not out.' But Eddie mutters to Acfield in the Lancashire accent of his, 'Just turn it one more inch, Ackers, and we'll get the bugger in a minute, you'll see.'

A famous benefit of doubt umpire is Harold 'Dickie' Bird – very hard for a bowler to get a narrow decision out of Dickie; ask any bowler the world over. Dear old Dickie. I can't remember whether it was Somerset v Northants at Taunton or at Northampton. However, Allan Lamb comes out to field and, after a couple of overs, he 'realises' he's got his mobile phone in his pocket, so he hands it to Dickie and asks if he'd mind putting it in his bigger pocket for the duration. Dickie refuses at first and starts a song and dance, complaining about modern players, new-fangled devices and what the world's coming to, but in the end he agrees and puts it down at the bottom of his ample great pocket.

A couple of overs later, just as the bowler is beginning his run-up from Dickie's end, in the pavilion Ian Botham is dialling a number ....

The phone rings shrilly in Dickie's pocket. Total consternation and blind panic from the umpire who is now dancing about like a cat on hot bricks, thinking he's got a hornets' nest in his pocket; utter panic and shellshock. The whole field collapsed in laughter.

GRAHAM GOODE

A Channel 4 racing commentator.

Q: What's the difference between the London Zoo and the Square Mile?
A: At the London zoo the animals are behind the bars.

* * *

A friend of mine is so worried about the taxman – when he pays you a compliment, he asks for a receipt.

A former England international cricketer who played 117 Test matches between 1978 and 1992. The elegant left-handed batsman scored 8,231 Test runs at an average of 44 and captained his country 32 times. He is now a cricket presenter and commentator.

When I captained England's tour to India in 1984–85 I was delighted to include in the squad a great friend of mine, Chris Cowdrey. Having initially earmarked him for a place in the one-day internationals, I picked him instead for all the Test matches. Eventually I needed to call up Chris to bowl at a time when Kapil Dev was in full flow and we set a suitably defensive field with only one man in the slips, Mike Gatting. After two or three balls I asked Chris if he would like Mike any wider at slip. His response: 'If he gets any wider, he'll burst.'

When Chris later bowled Kapil, his father, Colin, in his car in London, could not believe that Chris had been asked to bowl and had even taken Kapil Dev's wicket. He was so distracted that he drove the wrong way down a one-way street – the police were equally disbelieving and totally unsympathetic.

* * *

In 1986 in the West Indies we had a terrible time. Mike Gatting was our in-form batsman in the early weeks of the tour but then had his nose broken by a short-pitched delivery in the opening one-day international at Sabina Park. We sent him home to have his nose remodelled and the press met him at Heathrow. There was Mike with two panda-like black eyes and 2 two strips of tape on the bridge of his nose, a sort of 'X marks the spot.'

Unbelievably the first question was, 'So, where exactly did the ball hit you?' To his eternal credit, as he began to point to the injury site, Mike managed to laugh at the ludicrous question and even returned to the Caribbean to put his new nose back into the firing line later in the tour.

HEROL GRAHAM

*A former British and European Middleweight boxing
champion, he is also a former world title boxing challenger
at Middleweight and Super Middleweight.*

So everything's going amazingly well in my World Middleweight title fight with Julian Jackson. After four rounds the referee told my corner that they were going to pull Jackson out of the fight at the end of the fifth round ... and I would be World Champion. I was so excited when I got back to Brendan Ingle in the corner.

Then he took my gumshield out and all my dentures fell out with it. I couldn't believe it. My dentures in his hands. Still, the referee had said Jackson had one more round. Trouble was, so did I! I was knocked out cold in that fifth round. Maybe I have always been a little bit too concerned about my looks!

"WE DON'T NORMALLY STOP TO GIVE LIFTS, YOU KNOW"

*Maker of 100 centuries, this tall and elegant right-handed
cricketer was one of the finest and most watchable batsmen
produced by England since the Second World War. An
England international between 1951 and 1969, he played
74 Test matches and scored 4,882 runs at an average of 44,
including 11 centuries. He played for Worcestershire, and
captained Gloucestershire. Graveney was lately the president
of Worcestershire, and has forged a career as a successful
cricket broadcaster.*

In 1966, I made it back into the England team and had a good
run against the West Indians. I lived in the lovely town of
Winchcombe, between Cheltenham and Broadway. Our house
was on the main road and on Sunday I used to clean up outside. I was doing this when a couple of boys cycled by. The
bigger lad turned to his pal and said, 'Tom Graveney lives
there.'

The reply: 'Whereabouts?'

'Where that old fellow is sweeping up!'

* * *

After finishing playing I was fortunate enough to join the TV
commentary team at the BBC. During a Test at Edgbaston,
which in those days was a pretty slow low pitch, I was in the
box with Tony Lewis, who was the main commentator. Curtly
Ambrose was bowling to Graham Gooch and he let go a very
quick bouncer. I expected Tony to say something but he didn't
so I said, 'There, that goes to show he can get it up anytime he
wants!'

I had quite a post bag over the next couple of days.

LUCINDA GREEN

A former World and European Equestrian Champion, she won Badminton six times on six different horses and is an Olympic silver medallist.

At the prizegiving of an event, all crowded around the prize table with Princess Anne giving out the prizes, I burst my way to the front to collect what I had heard earlier was the first prize I had won – only to be told by PA when I finally got there that I had not won it anyway – a late result had been posted ....

* * *

I was being interviewed by the late Raymond Brooks-Ward for the BBC after winning the World Championships when an electric shock must have gone through the microphone and he dropped it – all on live television.

WILL GREEN

An England rugby union international prop, he made his debut in a 15–15 draw v Australia in 1997. He has won three caps so far and plays his club rugby for Wasps.

Before rugby went professional a few years ago, Wasps Vandals (second XV) were playing against Bracknell in a pre-season friendly. We didn't have a strong side out because of most of the team being away on their summer holidays.

Before the game the referee came in to the changing room to check studs and talk to the front rows to tell them the usual dribble about how he was going to referee. Except this time it was very different as the referee told us of his misfortune of the day before when he was working on a building site and fell off a ladder – causing him to be knocked unconscious.

He seemed fine so we got on with the game. After 20 minutes the referee was completely all over the place and collapsed. Our doctor ran on and managed to get him to his feet. After about five minutes or so he was insisting that he still wished to continue and finish the game.

Before he restarted play our captain went up to him and asked, 'Are you alright?'

'Yes,' he replied.

'Just to confirm the scoreline, Wasps 14, Bracknell 3.' In fact the true score was Wasps 3, Bracknell 14.

'Thanks captain,' the grateful referee responded.

So we carried on playing and Wasps scored a couple of tries and Bracknell added a couple more before half-time came. We had our oranges and just before we kicked off for the second half, the Bracknell captain asked the referee the score.

'Wasps 26, Bracknell 15.' All hell broke loose.

Our captain had to sheepishly own up to his dishonesty; the referee was enlightened with the true score.

Strangely enough, we didn't get the run of the referee in the second half and lost the game. Cheers, Skipper.

WILL GREENWOOD

An England rugby union international centre who has won 30 caps to date and is the third highest English try scorer of all time with 19 touchdowns. He was a Lions tourist to South Africa in 1997 and to Australia in 2001, and plays his club rugby at Harlequins.

Picture the scene, a Harlequins match, away to Munster. Quins had managed to get into the European competition and this was a crunch match. On Friday night everyone went to bed early, keen to prepare in the best possible way for this massive clash with the Irish, who were feeling confident on their home patch.

I was rooming with Tony Diprose [Dippers]; there we were, snoring away when there was a loud knock on the door. We ignored it. The insistent knocking continued, louder this time. I opened one eye, saw it was 7.30 in the morning so we didn't respond. Loud knocking again:

'This is the Police, open up.'

'Yeh, yeh, sure, p*** off, will you.'

'Open up immediately, there has been a murder,' came the reply.

'Very funny, now p*** off.' We were convinced it was a mate playing the fool. It then dawned on us that the voice didn't in any way sound familiar, and so slightly ruffled, Dippers rolled out of bed and opened the door. Standing there were two very serious-looking policemen.

'About time too, Sir,' looking at Dippers, 'There has been a murder, we would like to question you.'

'Oh God,' we thought, 'Who could it be, one of ours?'

The Chief Superintendent then pokes his head round the corner and says, 'Oh, hello Will, how are you doing?' totally forgetting the fact that he was on a man-hunt, and had just dropped a bombshell on us.

'Nice to welcome you to Munster, I'm sure there will be a warm reception for you at Thormond Park this afternoon.'

But my mind was still on the murder. Was it in the hotel? When did it happen? The policeman was having none of it.

'Anyway, the weather is due to be blustery, may be a hint of rain, wasn't it a great result for the Irish, beating you boys just recently?' And so on. This continued for about a quarter of an hour: outside centre running angles, referees, the tackle laws – the lot was up for discussion, but not the murder. Now, much as we were keen to help the police with their enquiries, we wanted our sleep. Eventually we politely managed to steer the conversation around to the murder, not rugby, to which he replied, 'Oh yes, that murder, it obviously wasn't you two, we know that, but lovely to chat. Oh and by the way, Munster will win today.'

He was right about the murder, it wasn't one of us and he was right about the result; we lost.

DANNY GREWCOCK

An England rugby union international second row who has won 33 caps to date. He was a Lions tourist in 1997 and 2001 and plays his club rugby for Bath, for whom he is captain.

The whole Lions squad were on a bus, travelling to a pre-tour dinner before we left for the Lions trip to Australia, 2001. It had been a heavy day's training, a full-on workout on a hot day, with heaps of energy expended, and loads of liquid drunk to keep the hydration levels up. It had taken its toll on different players in different ways. Rob Henderson was spark out, fast asleep, head back, mouth open – snoring away in his seat by the loo. I was outside the loo, waiting to attend to the call of nature. Lawrence Dallaglio was in there – doing his business. At that moment the driver, who obviously did not know the road very well, slammed on the brakes and flung the coach into a hard left to get around a corner.

Well, the latch was obviously not on the loo door properly. Lawrence was hurled back out of the door, hose in hand, still in mid-flow. Rob, who was still fast asleep, still snoring, mouth open, got the full spray all over him. The whole squad, who had seen this, erupted with laughter. Lawrence shot back into the loo, and I ducked behind a seat, keen not to be nailed by Henderson as the man responsible.

He was woken by the laughter and the feeling of dampness, not knowing what was going on.

'What the hell is this?' he said, looking down. 'Blimey, I'm pissed off.'

'Well, Hendo,' replies a voice, 'you've also been pissed on!'

SALLY GUNNELL

Sally Gunnell was the British heroine of the 1992 Olympics, winning a gold medal in the 400m Hurdles. Specialising in the 400m Hurdles and the 4 x 400m Relay, she won two gold medals in the 1990 Commonwealth Games and a silver (for the hurdles) in the 1991 World Championships. At the 1992 Olympics in Barcelona, as captain of the British women's team, Gunnell won the gold medal for the hurdles and a bronze for the relay. She is a former world record holder for the 400m Hurdles. Gunnell is now a reporter and presenter for BBC Athletics.

I met my husband Jon when we were both 19. He was the middle of three brothers; Chris was three years older and studying at Brighton Art College, Matt was four years younger and attending the local high school. Gradually throughout the summer I got to know the Bigg family very well, spending time in Brighton. We all got on very well and appeared to have the same sense of humour.

As Christmas approached there was talk as to how we would spend it. Christmas Day in Brighton was decided by us young-sters, and then there was the suggestion of fancy dress.

Well, I just knew straight away what I would dress as …. My Dad is a farmer in Essex and each year he breeds turkeys for the Christmas market. So when the day came for the turkeys to be plucked, I was to be found in the shed selecting only the finest feathers! I then spent several days sewing them on to a long-sleeved leotard, using the long tail-feathers along the arms to form wings. I planned to wear cream-coloured tights, a white swim cap and a cardboard beak. My outfit was complete – a Christmas turkey!

I managed to keep this a big secret from the Bigg boys. Whenever we met, there were big wind-ups as to what each was going to wear. Christmas Day dawned and I arrived in Brighton with my fancy dress hidden in a bag (a large bag). After Christmas dinner it was decided to hold the fancy dress parade with Jon's Mum and Dad as judges. So upstairs I went to change. It took quite a time to struggle into my feathered leotard – they are difficult enough at the best of times!

Tights on, swim hat on and finally the beak – off I went down the stairs, frightening Jon's cat in the process!

I burst into the living room only to find Jon and his broth-ers still in their ordinary clothes completely collapsed with laughter. They had had no intention whatsoever of dressing up, and had utterly taken me in all along! And there I was, in my leotard, completely encased in feathers!

You can imagine the laugh we had. It still amazes me that I stayed with Jon and even married him! Still, I must say that

I have got even with each one of those Bigg boys one by one. How? Well, that's another story.

REG GUTTERIDGE

Born into a fighting family in Islington, London in 1924, his grandfather (Arthur) was a renowned boxer, while his father (Dick) and uncle (Jack) were skilled trainers. Over the last 45 years, Reg has travelled the globe covering boxing for British audiences, and has become one of the most respected and popular commentators on the sport.

Heavyweight Nosher Powell often sparred with the great Joe Louis and also performed his losing contests at big London shows against Basil Kew. Nobody left the shows early.

When matched with a champion, Johnny Williams, after the fight Nosher was hauled before the Boxing Board of Control for – politely put – 'not giving his best'. He was accused of not being hit when going down.

'But he was bleeding going to!' pleaded Nosher.

H

KEITH HACKETT

—◆—

*A former FIFA international football referee who refereed
the 1981 FA Cup final between Tottenham Hotspur and
Manchester City.*

One of the finest matches I refereed in the early part of my
Football League career was between Sunderland and
Manchester United at Roker Park on Easter Monday, April
1977, during my second season as a Football League referee.
Sunderland won a truly rousing encounter 2–1. Tommy
Docherty, then the United manager, said afterwards in a radio
interview with Desmond Lynam, who was working for BBC
Radio at the time, 'The ref had a magnificent game.'

I felt 10 feet tall, even though the Sunderland manager
Jimmy Adamson was not pleased that I had taken the names of
two of his players, despite the fact that I also cautioned two
from United in an effort to ensure that the stirring match was
under my full control. As I left the ground, pleased that
Docherty thought I had helped contribute to a memorable
match, a young boy asked for my autograph. I reminded him
that I was the referee and not a player.

'I know,' was his reply. I gladly signed on a piece of paper, hesitating to ensure that my very first autograph was OK. I handed it over to the youngster, thanking him for asking me.

He then looked up at me and, as he tore it into small pieces, he said, 'Me Dad thinks you were rubbish.'

*　*　*

The oldest football ground in the world is situated in Sheffield at Sandygate Road where Hallam Football Club, the second oldest football club, still play their games.

I was appointed to officiate a County Senior Division Two game and was informed that I would have to provide my own linesmen.

The ground at Hallam has a huge slope and without linesmen it is difficult to judge offside decisions.

Just before kick-off, after several requests for volunteers to run the line, I got a knock on the door and after a quick conversation I ascertained that the only volunteer had two years' experience of running a line.

He seemed fully genned up on the laws, so I happily gave him authority to perform all the duties of a linesman, including, of course, flagging for offside.

In the opening minutes, he gave two or three offside decisions – which I checked by running opposite him. His judgement was spot-on. He clearly knew his stuff and I looked forward to an easier afternoon, having the rare privilege of at least one linesman in a County Senior game.

After 15 minutes, my expert linesman suddenly began flagging vigorously, waving his flag to attract my attention. I blew my whistle and stopped play and was immediately surrounded by a number of players unhappy with my decision. I ran over to the linesman, who was still flagging, thinking that a skirmish had taken place off the ball behind my back. I approached him, wondering how many players were going to be dismissed.

I started by asking for clarification as to why he was flagging. He appeared surprised that I had stopped play.

'Right, what's gone off and who are the players involved?' I asked.

He replied by informing me that he was flagging to attract the attention of his mate who had just entered the ground through the door at the top end of the ground. The players around me started laughing and, with a red face, I re-started play.

ANDREW HARRIMAN

An England rugby union international winger, who was one of the quickest players in the world in the early 1990s. He was captain of the World Cup-winning England 7s team in 1993.

When the England 7s squad left for Scotland for the 1993 World Cup as a group of unfancied and mainly unknown players, we arrived in Edinburgh on the night of a player's birthday. Damian Hopley is not the kind of person to let the small matter of a World Cup ruin his birthday, so a rather alcoholic night ensued.

Naturally our first day's training the next morning was rather unimpressive. England lost 21–0 to an unknown local district Under 21 7s team!!! The manager called me to one side: 'I've made a dreadful mistake in selecting the no. 6.'

I pleaded with him: 'Just give him one more chance.' I had after all had a great time drinking with him all night.

Lawrence Dallaglio got one more chance and has never looked back since!!!

◆

A professional darts player who was World Matchplay champion in 1998 and 1999. He acquired the nickname 'Prince of Style' when he became the first player to don a shirt and tie in an attempt to improve the sport's image.

While training my local football team, we were having shooting practice. The players were not taking it seriously so after half an hour I had the hump and said, 'If an old man like me can do it, you boys can pull your fingers out.'

I ran at the goalkeeper, beat him and from about 6 yards let rip with my left foot, only to hit the post. The ball flew back and hit me full in the face, splitting both lips and breaking my nose.

That didn't hurt, though. It was the squad laughing at me that was really painful.

I THINK THAT MAY HAVE BEEN FRACTIONALLY OUT

SMALL CLAIMS COURT

MILES HARRISON

A Sky TV rugby union commentator since 1994, Miles Harrison also commentates on tennis. He was previously with the BBC where he covered many football, tennis and rugby events.

Wales has always been the most passionate of rugby nations. In the 1960s, an 18-year-old full back left Monmouth School and walked straight into the national side to score a record 19 points against England on his debut in Cardiff. Fairy tales do come true. Wales' total of 34 points was a record versus the old enemy and, understandably, Keith Jarrett left the after-match dinner, clutching his new cap and wearing the broadest of smiles. The story goes that a driver of a single-decker bus saw the new national hero wandering in St Mary's Street after midnight, pulled up alongside him, wound the window down and said, 'Keith Jarrett – 19 points against England this afternoon, what a performance! What are you doing walking the streets of Cardiff at this time?'

Jarrett replied, 'Well, to tell you the truth, I haven't a lift home.'

'Get in,' the driver said, 'I'll take you – where do you live?'

Jarrett tentatively suggested, 'Newport,' and the driver told him he'd have to clear it with his inspector at the depot. When the driver tried to explain to his boss that he wanted to take the bus all the way to Newport, the inspector would have none of it.

'But, Guv,'said the driver, 'the guy in the bus is Keith Jarrett who helped Wales beat England at the Arms Park today.'

'Put that bus away!' cried the inspector. 'Get a double-decker out – he might want a smoke!'

* * *

Over the years, I have made many a *faux pas* at the micro-phone, whatever the sport! Here is one such exchange, which still makes me smile to this day.

It's a hot afternoon on Centre Court at Wimbledon and in the BBC Radio commentary box the temperature is rising. The match is between Scandinavia's Stefan Edberg and Kenneth Carlsen. I close my commentary with my mind having clearly drifted away to thoughts of a well-deserved drink: 'So that completes a fine straight sets victory for Carlsberg.'

John Inverdale: 'Thanks Miles. We've just witnessed "Probably the best tennis player in the world!"'

GUY HARWOOD

A racehorse trainer who spent 30 years in the sport training over 2,000 winners over the flat and jumps. His most famous winner was Dancing Brave who won the Arc de Triomphe in 1986.

I had a very nice owner who had a horse in training with me and lived very close to Goodwood racecourse. Not surprising, therefore that he was very anxious to run his horse at the main Goodwood meeting at the end of July. Unfortunately there was a problem: the horse in question really did not have much natural ability and certainly not enough to grace Goodwood at the main meeting. However, there was no way of telling the owner that the horse was not good enough or disappointing him by not running his horse at his local and favourite meeting.

The day before the meeting I found to my pleasure that Willie Carson was available. I therefore approached Willie with the offer of the ride, on the clear understanding that I was well aware that the horse was not good enough, but I didn't want Willie getting off his horse at the end of the race saying the horse was no good and so spoiling the owner's day. The instructions were to try and beat one other horse rather than trying to win the race and finishing tailed-off last. The last instruction was the most important: he was to get off the horse at the end of the race in the area that we used to dub 'excuses corner', and find something positive to say about the horse to the owner.

Willie gave the horse a hell of a ride, beat two other horses and came back to 'excuses corner'. He jumped off the horse, took his saddle off, and approached the owner.

'What did you think, Willie?' the owner asked expectantly.

'You know, Sir,' Willie replied with his broad Scottish grin, 'your horse is a lovely colour!'

Job well done!

GAVIN HASTINGS

Former Scotland rugby union international captain who played for his country 61 times between 1986 and 1995. He won the 1990 Grand Slam, beating England in the final game, and is Scotland's all-time leading points scorer with 667. He was a Lions tourist in 1989, then captain of the Lions in 1992 on the tour to New Zealand.

During the 1987 World Cup in New Zealand we were all watching the news on TV one night and the newscaster was reading out the weather temperatures for towns throughout New Zealand:

Auckland 20	Wellington 18
Christchurch 14	Invercargill 10
Palmerston North 16	Wangaum 12

One of the guys, a prop, walks into the team room and looks at the TV, then exclaims, 'Crikey, these scores are pretty close!'

SCOTT HASTINGS

A Scotland rugby union international and Lions tourist in 1989 and 1993, he is the second most capped Scottish player of all time, winning 65 caps.

Scotland won the Grand Slam in 1990 and the SRU organised a celebration dinner in the company of HRH The Princess Royal. During the dinner I went up to Princess Anne and asked her for the microphone.

In front of the team and 200 others, I said, 'Excuse me, Ma'am, but there is one question that has not been answered … Jenny Ovens, will you marry me?'

Luckily she said yes and we have two wonderful kids and 12 years of marriage behind us.

ROB HAWTHORNE

Rob Hawthorne joined Sky Sports from BBC Radio 5 at the start of the 1995–96 to commentate on the Premier League in Monday Night Football. *One year later he commentated on Sky's first season of live coverage of the Nationwide Football League. He has now come full circle as he returns to Premier League football on Monday nights.*

For some years now, I have covered the Republic of Ireland's international matches for both radio and television, so it was particularly gratifying when at a recent West Ham match last season, I was approached by an Irish fan wanting to shake my hand. 'I've always wanted to meet you,' he said. 'You're a legend in Ireland … What's your name again?'

* * *

A leading manager told me the true story of when he once took a team to Grimsby. In the hotel bar, discussing tactics with his coaching staff on the eve of the game, they were descended upon by a party of women. Keen to find out the nature of the occasion, he asked one if it was a hen party or something.

'No,' she replied, 'it's a Weight Watcher's convention.'

'Oh, not been going long?' he asked casually, at which point she floored him with her best right hook.

ALEX HAY

A former Ryder Cup referee, best known for his golf commentary on the BBC, where he has broadcast since 1978.

Watching golf by satellite is something we in Britain now take for granted.

Throughout the year from all around the globe we can enjoy endless hours, in spite of countless advertising breaks, with the world's best competing.

Much of this success is due to the early efforts of a small television company by the name of Screensport which – prior to losing out its American golf events with the advent of Sky and finally its European coverage to Eurosport – provided those in the British Isles and large parts of Europe, who had access to a dish or cable, with a full coverage of live international golf.

It is remarkable that only around a decade or so ago no one knew if this would work, so the Screensport Team were quite adventurous. For the first two or three years, prior to European coverage coming on board, the viewing audience was only treated to American golf. The pictures came by satellite but the commentators, contrary to the beliefs of the audience, came by car, for the joining of both took place in a cellar not far from Carnaby Street In London.

I, along with Dave Brenner, made up the commentary team. Leaving my office at Woburn Golf Club by 5 p.m., I could be in my seat awaiting the satellite's arrival over the horizon, which was usually around 7.30. By 1 a.m. I would be on my way home up the M1.

So, from Thursday to Sunday this became my way of life.

Never once did we lie and claim to be there, we simply received from America the Draw sheet, the yardage of the holes and added the odd bit of dialogue to the pictures and left the rest to the viewers' imaginations. We gathered a huge fanmail from people who envied our travels, telling us how fortunate we were to mix with the great players.

As our confidence grew and to the annoyance of our director, we gave up listening to any guide commentary. The commercial breaks of the Americans, plus our own, as well as two lots of directors was unbearable so we preferred to 'wing it', so thinking on one's feet, or seat in this case, became part of the game.

We began turning up later and the producer would have

compiled some nice pictures to talk over which we did until something happened.

On one such evening, first night of the Tucson Open, there had been delays and some problems so the pictures would be late. Never mind, we had a few scenes from the previous year's coverage which were slipped in as we 'went to air'. We waxed on about the new desert course, how everyone had enjoyed seeing it last year – a magnificent layout miles from anywhere with not a building in sight, with the only vegetation some cactus and tumbleweed.

The usual comments were made about the strengths of the players, the toughest holes, all the usual waffle for we had no drawsheets, no yardages, the faxes from the Tournament Office were down.

At last! The director: 'We have pictures, cue commentators.'

Tom Watson was making his way onto the tee. Thank the Lord, someone we knew. Behind the tee was a fairly large villa.

'Dave, isn't it amazing how the success of golf brings prosperity. There wasn't a building to be seen a year ago and just look at that beautiful home.'

'Yes,' replied Dave.' It's been the same story all over Spain and Portugal. Build a good course and houses just spring up.'

'Information, guys, Watson is on the 12th tee and four under,' the director says.

Dave (with the benefit of his notes from a year ago):

'Alex, this is a pretty tough little par three – difficult club selection?'

'Yes,' hedging my bets … 'probably between a seven and an eight iron. If the head is rounded you make it an eight, if straight then a seven.'

Anyway at 6000 miles nobody would notice the difference. Dave was pointing at our monitor, Tom Watson had reached over to his golf bag, his hand was on one of his long irons.

'They were talking of lengthening some of the short holes,

unless of course he is going to punch one under the desert wind, you know how clever he was on our links courses.' Not bad, I thought, got out of that one.

'Alex, why is Tom taking a Wood?'

Quick as a flash: 'It must be this desert wind.'

'From a seven to a driver?'

'No, David, he's going to measure two club lengths, the maximum amount he is allowed to go back on the tee! He likes to get it just right.'

At that point the cameras backed up to reveal not just one home but a whole estate.

'Goodness, they've built these quickly, we said it was a great venue.'

The cameraman continued to back out. Into the picture came a skyscraper, then another and along with it the director's voice: 'OK, commentators, we've just received a fax, the Desert Course was washed out by a flash-flood yesterday and they've moved onto the City Course.'

At that point Tom Watson unleashed a full-blooded drive, the director continued, 'For your information, on this course the 12th measures 600 yards. Now let's hear you talk your way out of that one!'

EDDIE HEMMINGS

Sky TV's lead rugby league commentator and presenter, he is the face and voice of Sky rugby league in partnership with Michael Stephenson. Since 1991, Eddie has been involved with the full range of rugby league programming, including weekly live matches from the Tetleys Super League, two Rugby League World Cups and the best in Australian rugby league.

Working with a bloke like 'Stevo' [Mike Stephenson] on TV is rather like walking blindfold through a minefield! I never know what he's going to come out with next ... and in the 11 years we've been together covering Rugby League on Sky Sports, we have had some 'pearlers'.

Eleven years working with one colleague is a bit like a marriage, isn't it? Come to think of it, if I'd shot him back then I'd be out now .... But I digress. We have had a myriad of catch phrases over the years ... 'It's TRY TIME' he roars whenever there's one scored but his critical analysis of key plays is what Stevo has built his reputation on. Examples are:

'He's got a smile as wide as Christmas Day' (please can someone explain that one?) and 'It's a simple fact. If you earn bread-and-butter money you can't live on prawns!' But the all-time classics include 'Adrian Morley (Leeds Rhinos) hit him with all the power of an EXERCISE missile!!!!' and 'Sean Long (St Helens goal-kicker) has kicked 43 goals this season so far. That's exactly TWICE AS MANY as he scored last year.'

You simply cannot make these up – they actually happened and went out on air. My favourite STEVO-BALLS, though, came the day that we were covering a St Helens Super League match at Knowsley Road. Saints had had most of the play but for some inexplicable reason kept dropping the ball near the try line. I turned to my learned colleague and said, 'You know, Stevo, Saints must have dropped the ball at least five times tonight with the line at their mercy ...' Then came the reply. 'Oh no, Eddie it's more than that. I'd put it into double figures. I think they've dropped the ball NINE times already ....' Needless to say it's great fun ... never a dull moment ... and long may it continue!!!!

A former Middlesex and Surrey cricketer, he has more recently been the Charterhouse School cricket professional.

HM the Queen was scheduled to visit Charterhouse School in the summer of 1971. The preparations were extensive and required the provision of an exclusive toilet facility for HM.

The task of redecorating and installing a new WC, etc. in one of the boarding houses, fell to a quiet and well-respected old retainer on the maintenance staff. His royal commission completed, he joined his mates for their regular afternoon tea break, which always included a card session. He was teased considerably and asked whether this was the pinnacle of his long serving employment.

As the first poker hand was dealt, he brought the house down: 'Well, I suppose that's the nearest I will ever get to a Royal Flush.'

(As the then cricket professional at Charterhouse I met the Queen and confess it was a miracle that I only managed to express a polite smile as we shook hands.)

ALISTAIR HIGNELL

*An England rugby union international player gaining
14 caps between 1975 and 1979, he also played county
cricket for Gloucester between 1974 and 1983. He is
currently a BBC radio rugby commentator.*

Rugby's come a long way since the days – over a quarter of a century ago now – when I was fortunate enough to wear the white shirt of England. In those days, Twickenham was a ramshackle old stadium, we got together for a run-around on a Thursday afternoon, and had Friday off – not so much in accordance with a regime designed to enable us to reach peak performance at the right time, but because the lads needed time to get their cars into central London where the post-match dinner was to be held. But things were changing. We had a team doctor, but not for away tours – one of the reserves was a medical student, and he could look after us – only half the selectors still believed that a coach was a four-wheeled vehicle to get you to the stadium. Now of course the England set-up is awash with experts: attacking coaches, defensive coaches, kicking coaches, throwing-in coaches, head coaches, dieticians, sports psychologists, fitness coaches, kinesiologists – the lot. And no expense is spared in the use of these guys – and any other agency that might give England the edge. Manager Clive Woodward's admiration for the Royal Marines is well-documented. The England team often found themselves down at Lympstone in South Devon where the mental and physical training was designed to bond them into a unit as tight and fearsome as the Marines themselves.

One such exercise involved orienteering on Bodmin Moor. As always, the England players were thoroughly briefed by their Marine instructors before being sent off in pairs, with instructions on where to camp overnight and where to report the following morning. Jason Leonard was paired with Jerry Guscott. With great difficulty the two had found the first few checkpoints and the spot where they were due to spend the night. After sharing out the hardtack, they settled into their tent, only to be disturbed by a low growling noise coming from just outside.

'What's going on?' asked Jeremy – obviously in training for his later role as a television analyst. Soon they could make out a massive four-legged shape outside the tent. 'Oh hell!' said Jase, 'I reckon it's what the Marines warned us about – it's the Beast of Bodmin – as such.' Jerry started to tie up his trainers and struggle into his sweat-top.... 'SSSH!,' hissed Jase. 'Remember the Marines said our only chance was to keep absolutely quiet, and hope he goes away!' Jerry finished dressing, and lifted up the back flap of the tent.

'What on earth are you doing?' whispers Jase. 'You know what the Marines said.'

'I'm going to run for it,' calmly replies Jerry.

'Are you mad?' hisses Jase. 'Don't you remember what they said ... no one can outrun the beast of Bodmin!'

'I know that,' says Jerry, 'but I can sure as hell outrun you, you great lardass!'

* * *

However tawdry the bidding process, however involved the shenanigans in the actual awarding of the Olympic Games, when the event actually comes around, it never fails to remind of the good things in sport – the dedication, the commitment, the noble sacrifices, the honest endeavour, the twin impostors of victory and failure, the shared goal, the camaraderie of the young sportspeople involved. Picture then the scene in the cafeteria at the athletes' village, mid-way through the games. One competitor attempts to enter into the family spirit of the games. 'I hope you don't mind me asking,' he enquires of the man in front of him in the queue, 'but are you a pole-vaulter?'. The man turns to him, 'No, I'm German, but how did you know my name?'

RICHARD HILL

─────── •◆• ───────

An England rugby union flanker, often portrayed as the silent assassin at both club and international level. His effective and abrasive style of forward play has made him legendary in rugby circles. Hill made his England debut back in February 1997 in a 41–13 triumph over Scotland at Twickenham and has gained 49 caps to date. He was a Lions tourist to South Africa in 1997 and to Australia in 2001.

Back in the amateur days, under the floodlights at Saracens' training ground, training was suddenly stopped. Under the instruction of Dave Brain, a second row forward, we were spaced out across the width of the pitch and told to look down. Then on command we were told to walk forward and look for his missing object. Take into account that this pitch was in the middle of a council-owned park.

We were looking for his false tooth that had fallen out sometime during the session, but he was unsure when.

Positives? Less training. Did we find the tooth? No chance.

* * *

One Saracens v Bristol game was a particularly muddy affair, mid-winter on the Southgate pitch. After the game a boot-bath, full of cold mud, was placed next to the communal bath. It was tradition to leave a space in the corner for poor unsuspecting victims who would have the boot-bath emptied on them.

On this occasion, it was the turn of Kyran Bracken, then of Bristol, to thank the occupants of the bath gratefully for moving over to leave a space in the corner for him.

As he was seen to duck under the water to tend his then complete head of pristine hair, Mark Burrows exited to empty the boot-bath. To Kyran's shock, he surfaced, mouth open, as the discoloured water hit him. Schoolboy error!

RICHARD HILL

— ◆ —

England rugby union scrum half, winning 29 caps. A World Cup finalist in 1991, he played club rugby for Bath where he helped the club to 8 Cup Final wins and six League titles in 11 years.

Stuart Barnes, in a previous life before Sky TV, was the manager of a building society. He was in work one day, as usual in his office in the centre of Bath. His three lady cashiers were working hard at the front desk, and Stuart was keeping an eye on proceedings in his office with his two closed-circuit monitors.

The girls at the counter were suddenly confronted by a

masked gunman, demanding money over the counter. The three girls bravely tried to stall the gunman, playing for time. After all, they thought, the tough, brave England rugby player Mr Barnes would soon charge from his desk and rescue the three girls in distress. They waited … and waited – no Stuart – no saviour.

They eventually had to give the gunman the money and he charged off. The three girls were trembling after their ordeal, in a state of shock, still no Stuart. Where was their boss and hero? They found him, not *behind* his desk, but underneath it!

SIMON HODGKINSON

An England rugby union international full back, gaining
14 caps between 1989 and 1991, he played his club rugby
for Nottingham.

Scotland v England, 1990, the Grand Slam decider. Just before the anthems, we were pumped up to the max, desperate to get stuck into the Scots, all the usual characters: Brain Moore, Wade Dooley, Mike Teague, Peter Winterbottom, Mick Skinner, all lined up waiting for the battle to begin.

Just before the anthems were to be played, Princess Anne came down with her two children, Peter and Zara Phillips. Will Carling was doing the honours: 'Brian Moore – Ma'am – Paul Rendall, Jeff Probyn, Paul Ackford', etc., etc.

'Hello, hello, hello, best of luck,' came the reply, in her perfect Queen's English. The thing was, she was wearing tartan, as were her two children who were following behind, shaking hands as well. It was quite obvious whom they wanted to win.

She had just got to me, thirteenth or so in the line when there was a muffled yelp from further back down the row. Princess Anne, Will Carling and most of the English team turned around to see where the scream had come from.

We saw who from, and why. Wade Dooley, who like the rest of us, was ready to knock anything Scottish into next week, had little Peter Phillips who was about twelve or thirteen at the time, by the hand, and was squeezing mercilessly during the handshake.

Big Wade Dooley – the first Englishman to get stuck into a Scot that day.

CARL HOGG

A Scotland rugby union international flanker, Hogg made his debut v Australia in 1992, gaining five caps in all.

It was 1992 – Scotland's tour to Australia, and I had just been selected for my first cap. It was a dream come true, to play for my country was all I had ever wanted. Here I was, just about to take on the finest side in the world, in their back yard – it was simply the ultimate challenge.

The Ozzies like to do things with a bit of drama, there were flags everywhere, XXXX dancing girls parading around; the scene was set for this huge clash.

Out we ran, lined up and 'Flower of Scotland' began to play. This was a hugely emotional time for me, I could hardly see through the tears. I started belting out the words, filled with pride. Next to me was Doddie Weir.

'Oh Flower of Scotland ...'

Doddie interrupted: 'Look at them, little do they know what they are in for later.'

'I'm with you Dod,' I replied.

'We are going to get stuck into them,' said Doddie.

'Damn right,' I replied. 'When will we see ...' The anthem continued.

'Oh Hoggy, they are not going to know what hit them.'

'Yup, we are going to f***ing smash them right up.' I was beside myself with passion.

'What?" said Doddie, now looking at me. 'What are you talking about?'

'Those Ozzies, come the first whistle, we are going to flatten them, destroy them.'

The anthem was still playing.

'No, you fool,' said Doddie. 'I wasn't talking about getting stuck into the Ozzies, open your eyes, I'm talking about the XXXX girls in front of us.'

DAMIAN HOPLEY

*An England rugby union international, he won the 1993
7s World Cup with England, and is now the Chief Executive
of the Professional Rugby Players' Association.*

I was playing for Wasps in an unusually close derby game against our glamorous south west London rivals, Harlequins. Our regular scrum half, Steve Bates, had cried off with an ankle injury on the morning of the game. Amid a shortage of no. 9s, our fourth choice half back, Chris Wright, got called up. Despite a good warm-up, it was soon apparent that he was not enjoying the best of games as nerves got the better of him on the big occasion. He was knocking balls on at the base of the scrum, and continually took the wrong option. Add to that a dreadful service that was comparable to Virgin Rail in its darkest days, and you can understand the frustration that the underused back line were experiencing.

Just before half-time, as our forwards made the hard yards up the field, 'Wrighty', (or should that have been 'Wrongy'?) took the ball on up yet another blind alley, only to find Peter Winterbottom standing in his way. He was spear-tackled head first into the ground by the England flanker and the entire crowd winced at the sound of the little fellow being pile-driven into the mud.

As he lay there on the ground groaning and groggy, the club physio, Sue Boardman, ran onto the field to treat him. After a few whiffs of the smelling salts, our scrum half was still struggling to come to terms with his surroundings. Sue Boardman turned to our talismanic captain Dean Ryan and said, 'It's no good Dean, he doesn't know who he is.' After pausing for a couple of seconds, Ryan replied, 'Then tell him he's Gareth Edwards.'

TIM HORAN

———————•◆•———————

An Australian rugby union international centre, he is the third most capped Australian of all time with 80 caps. He was part of the Australian World Cup-winning sides of 1991 and 1999.

In the 1991 World Cup we were very lucky to have an amazing amount of support from well-wishers, not just the fans who cheered us on our way but many who sent various messages to the team hotel – all were much appreciated. Well, we had managed to get to the World Cup final and were camped in our hotel, and to pass the time when not fine-tuning our game we went to the team room. It had literally hundreds of faxes and letters which were split into two areas – team messages and messages for individuals.

The messages were quite extraordinary: offers of free accommodation at five star hotels, free evenings at massage parlours, free beach holidays – anything and everything. It was flattering and sometimes amusing to check out these faxes. One evening Marty Roebuck was flipping through the new faxes when he came across a belter. A girl from Adelaide had faxed in: 'To whoever scores the first try in the final, I will offer you fantastic free sex.'

Below she put her phone number!

The game started and the first break in the match happened to come from me. I was haring down the right-hand side with only Will Carling between myself and the try line, also at stake this questionable offer should I be the first one to score the first try.

I decided to chip through – the ball went into touch ....

From the ensuing line-out we managed to pilfer possession, and the forwards drove over the line. The two props – Ewen McKenzie and Tony Daley – were both holding the ball, and crashed over the whitewash to score this crucial first try.

Rumour has it that five seconds later, the Adelaide lady disconnected her phone!

* * *

I was playing for the Queensland Reds in the Super 12 and were on a mini tour in South Africa. We had played the Stormers and were training down in Cape Town. Our next opponents were the Blue Bulls at altitude at a town called Brakpan. A TV journalist came up and asked our full back and the now Australian international Chris Latham for an interview. We were all wandering around and happened to listen in.

'No problem mate, fire away.'

'How do you think your form is at the moment?'

'Yeh, I'm pretty happy the way things are going. The team is playing well.'

'And a good performance against the Stormers ...'

'Yeh, we were happy the way things are progressing, annoyed to have lost by just a couple of points but are concentrating on the next match.'

'So what do you know about Brakpan?'

'Well I reckon he has a pretty good step and a tidy mispass …'

Embarrassment for the journalist: 'Sorry Chris, but can we do that last bit again, Brakpan is actually the place where you are playing ….'

We were of course all listening – BIG mistake from Latham!

MARK HOWELL

Judo coach and canoeing enthusiast.

While out weekend canoeing with some friends, Rhys unfortunately broke his little finger. After persuading him that the weekend would be spoilt spending time in an Accident and Emergency Department, we carried on canoeing for the remainder of the weekend.

At 1.30 in the early hours on Monday morning I received a phone call from Rhys: 'Mark, I've broken my finger, and now can't go mountain biking tomorrow.'

I was slightly confused: 'I know your finger is broken, I was there!'

Rhys replied, 'Well after our weekend away canoeing I attended A and E, they set my little finger and strapped it to my wedding finger. However, while I was out having a drink with some friends, the barman opened and dropped the hatch on my hand, re-breaking the little finger and breaking my wedding finger at the same time.'

* * *

While visiting my sister I decided to go and watch my nephews playing judo. To my great surprise there were several parents present whom I had taught judo over the years. We all stood at the side of the mat talking about old times and how it was much harder and tougher when we were doing judo. During a

146

break the instructor came over to this small but select group and asked, 'Everything OK?'

I replied, 'We were talking about old times and how we all started doing judo in this very room.'

The instructor then proceeded to ask, 'Had we had done judo with Mark Howell? He was a right hard b*****d and was very strict when on the mat and took no prisoners.'

There was an embarrassed silence from us all before I replied, 'I am Mark Howell!!'

" Where have you been I've MISSED you?"

ROB HOWLEY

◆

The most capped Welsh international rugby union scrum half of all time, winning 59 caps, and a Lions tourist in 1997 and 2001.

A rugby associate who shall be referred to as Player 'D' was a member of the Wales national team was selected in the squad for the Wales A v England A game at Wrexham.

Due to the long journey, the squad took a pit stop in

Welshpool for lunch and many ordered 'Soup of the Day', including our infamous Player 'D'.

As the waitress was serving the soup to the squad, Player 'D' decided to lean over to grab the condiments to shake onto his soup. The waitress seeing him, kindly remarked, 'I would taste it first love, if I was you!'

Player 'D' nonchalantly shook the pepper onto his wrist and took a lick!

WILL HOY

A professional racing driver who competed in the World Sports Car Championship, including six Le Mans races and various saloon car championships, winning the Japanese and the British Touring Car Championship.

Many strange, scary and amusing things happen to you in motor sport. One that was all of these and which was the most attention grabbing was in practice for a round of the British Touring Car Championship at the British Grand Prix circuit at Brands Hatch in my factory Williams Renault. I was on a very fast section at the back of the circuit when the steering felt strange, so I gave the steering wheel a tug (as you do!) and it came off in my hands. I'm now doing well over 100 m.p.h. at this point and approaching a corner without the benefit of a steering wheel is not a good predicament! The wheel has a quick-release mechanism that fits onto a spring and I had to line it up in the right place before being able to push it back on. Braking hard without a steering wheel would almost certainly have pitched me off the track, so it was my only choice. I got the wheel back on with about 20m of space!

I

JOHN INVERDALE

A radio and television presenter who has been at the cutting edge of BBC broadcasting for over 15 years. Inverdale is a former presenter of Radio Five Live's Sport on Five _and_ BBC TV's Rugby Special _among many other programmes._

A golfer was standing on the first tee and hits his opening drive straight at a tree. The ball ricochets backwards, hits him on the head, and kills him. He gets to the Pearly Gates, where St. Peter says to him, 'What are you here for?'

'One,' he replies.

* * *

And a true story.

I once had to interview Harry Carpenter for BBC Radio Lincolnshire.

I'd been at the BBC for about a month, and was extremely nervous about meeting the man who had been the voice of boxing for so long, and whom I'd grown up listening to. So nervous in fact, that we did the entire interview with me having put no tape in the tape recorder.

After chatting with him for more than ten minutes, I thanked him for his time, wiped the sweat from my brow, and walked out to the car. Just before driving off, I thought I'd better check that everything had worked OK. Imagine my horror when I realised I had recorded precisely nothing.

I had to decide whether to face the embarrassment of owning up to Harry, and asking him to do it again, or getting back to the office and admitting my error to my workmates.

Honesty was the best policy. I went back to Harry, told him what had happened, he looked at me as though I clearly had no future in the industry, graciously did it all over again, and I left much relieved. Funny now. Not remotely funny at the time.

J

BRIAN JACKS

*Jacks is a former British and European judo champion and
Olympic bronze medallist. His winning appearances on the
hugely successful British and European* Superstars *series
turned him into a household name.*

Fred is digging a hole in his garden. Bill from next door looks
over and says, 'What are you doing Fred?'
  'I'm burying my goldfish.'
  'It's a big hole Fred.'
  'Yes, it's inside your cat.'

STEVE JAMES

*The Glamorgan and England opening batsman made his
Test debut against South Africa at Lord's in 1998 in the
second Test. He has scored over 15,000 first class runs at an
average of over 40, with a top score of 309 not out.*

This is a true story about Darren Thomas, the Glamorgan
quick bowler. He was asked to arrange a team meal in

Liverpool back in 1997. Needing ideas, he decided to seek assistance from the receptionist.

He eventually surprised us by announcing that we were off to a French restaurant – called something like 'Maissez-vous.' Well, the night arrived and the taxi driver seemed a bit confused as to our destination but eventually pointed to a place, which turned out to be a Beefeater ... 'with a merry view!'

* * *

I was playing rugby for my home club Lydney in a Gloucestershire Cup Final against a side called Matson, who are renowned for their physicality. Sure enough a free-for-all developed from the kick-off. I was playing full back and never really enjoyed the physical stuff, so I stayed out of the way and it was just me and their full back, a chap called Les Jones (he also played for Gloucester and Pontypool) left. He came striding towards me and I feared the worst, bracing myself for the inevitable punch, but instead he said, 'Fancy an arm wrestle, James?'

Relief!!!

CHARLES JEFFREY

Captain of Chelsea Nomads Cricket Club.

While on tour in Gloucestershire a couple of years ago, the Chelsea Nomads were playing a fixture against Naunton CC, when there was a 'trouser incident.'

The Chelsea Nomads, whose members include Stuart Rodger and the late Nicholas Clay, fielded an overseas player from Australia, who rejoiced in the name of Fritter.

Fritter had forgotten to pack his cricket trousers and was obliged to resort to the club kit bag for clothing. The only available trousers were a drawstring-less pair, into which you could have fitted two Fritters.

The CNCC were in the field striving to take a crucial wicket with Fritter fielding at mid-wicket. The batsman we were trying to remove miscued a sweep shot, sending the ball at a steepling trajectory over Fritter's head. Fritter gamely turned and sprinted to catch the ball as it headed towards the boundary, thus offering the rest of the team a rear view as events unfolded. As he turned, the arrangement that Fritter had employed to hold up the commodious trousers gave away, so then did the trousers. The trousers had to be manually held in position as the ball started its descent to earth.

Fritter was well positioned to take the catch while running towards the boundary. As the ball and Fritter converged, he put his hands out to take the catch – immediately the trousers headed south – so both hands had to be employed to maintain their position at his waist. As the gap narrowed between Fritter and the ball, both hands were again thrust forward to receive the ball but again the trousers obeyed gravity and again both hands had to be re-employed at the waistband.

This process was repeated two or three times in rapid succession until the ball was tantalisingly close to being plucked out of the air. Fritter decided to go for broke. Ignoring the descent of the trousers, he reached, both arms outstretched, to catch the ball.

The trousers rapidly hit ground level trapping Fritter's ankles. There was instant locking of the legs causing Fritter to hit the ground face first, unchecked, with arms reaching forward and the ball thudding into the ground some six inches in front of his desperately outstretched fingers.

Not Out.

NEIL JENKINS

The most capped Welsh rugby union international of all time with 86 caps. He is also the most capped fly half in the history of the game and the highest points scorer the sport has ever known with 1,029 points to date.

Pontypridd RFC have always enjoyed a huge crowd of supporters. Indeed, the ritual chanting can have a very positive effect. My brother-in-law is an ardent Ponty supporter and often warms the crowd up with a plastic sheep-kicking routine. The players, one particular big game, were in the dressing room psyching themselves up for kick-off.

We were expecting an amazing reception from the crowd as the noise from the stand was deafening.

Well, the cheering was not for us but for Dolly – a real pet sheep who was running amok and fertilising the field with Andrew, in hot pursuit, unable to control her.

We fleeced the opposition, they were like lambs to the slaughter!

PADDY JOHNS

A former Ireland rugby union international and captain, he is the fourth most capped Irish international of all time with 59 caps.

This is a second-hand story I heard from an Ulster team-mate who played at Northampton. Three Northampton players were in the physio room before a game and were discussing company cars that they wanted to hire as their club cars.

The first player says, 'I want a BMW 3 series.'

The second player responds, 'I'm going for a Rover myself.'

The physio turns to the third player and says, 'I think you need a cortisone injection.'

The third player replies, 'No way, I want a Rover too.'

* * *

The St Marys and Ireland player, Trevor Brennan, was a member of the Irish rugby team staying at the Glenview Hotel in Wicklow. Trevor went to bed the night before the first training session at 10.30 p.m.. Training was scheduled for 9.30 a.m., after a short lift on the bus to the local ground in Greystones. Trevor woke up the following morning and looked at his watch. It was 11.30. Trevor panicked, and ran down the corridor to reception, dressing as he ran. When he got to reception he was out of breath.

Trevor: 'Can you please phone me a taxi!? I'm late for training.'

Receptionist: 'What do you mean, Trevor? It's only 5.30 a.m.'

Trevor's watch had stopped at 11.30 *PM*, an hour after going to bed.

IAN JONES

A New Zealand rugby union international, he is the second most capped All Black of all time with 79 caps.

The All Blacks were playing England, and after the half-time whistle blew they found they were ahead 56–0, Jonah Lomu getting eight tries. The rest of the team decided to head for the pub instead of playing the second half, leaving Jonah to go out for the second half on his own.

'No worries,' Jonah told them. 'I'll join you later and tell you what happened.'

After the game Jonah headed for the pub where he told his team-mates the final score: 95–3.

'What??!!!' said the furious captain. 'How did you let them get three points??!'

Jonah replied apologetically, 'I was sent off with 20 minutes to go.'

SALLY JONES

A former world real tennis champion and Britain's first net-worked woman TV sport presenter.

While working as a presenter on a regional news programme, my co-presenter, a much loved veteran broadcaster, would have no truck with the new fangled ear-pieces, preferring to take directions from the floor manager. He also spent the time after he had introduced a filmed report engrossed in *The Sporting Life* and busily picking his nose.

One day the film broke seconds after he had linked to it and the only camera in the studio immediately cut back to him, with his finger (of course) half-way up his nostril, quite unaware that that he was going out live to millions. We desperately waved and coughed in a vain bid to attract his attention.

The seconds dragged agonisingly and all I could hear in my own earpiece was the despairing voice of our editor in the control gallery, pleading hysterically:

'Phil, Phil Hughes, man, for pity's sake, don't eat it!'

* * *

As an inexperienced young broadcaster, I was horrified by the number of improper suggestions from viewers whose minds were obviously focused on other sports than the ones I was reporting. It was, then, a welcome relief one day to get an immaculately written letter on headed paper from a teenage boy.

He announced that he was my number one fan, and enjoyed my broadcasts because of my professionalism, expertise, calm authority, etc. (I preened myself). He was, he revealed, a shy young man, still living at home with his parents, and would I please not let them know he had written this. He remained my most devoted admirer, etc. then followed the most devastating PTO.

I turned the page … PS – Please will you send me a pair of your knickers?

K

CHRIS KAMARA

—◆—

A former professional footballer with Portsmouth, Swindon,
Brentford, Stoke, Leeds, Luton, Middlesbrough, Bradford,
Leeds and Sheffield United. He was also manager of
Bradford City and Stoke. He is now a Sky TV analyst.

I enjoyed a long career as a football player, signing for
Portsmouth (twice), Swindon (twice), Brentford, Stoke, Leeds,
Luton, Middlesbrough, Sheffield United and Bradford. I then
made the transition into football management at Bradford and
Stoke. One of my proudest moments as a manager was leading
the Bradford team out onto the Wembley pitch where we won
the Second Division play-off and gained promotion to the
First Division. Fantastic day!

I became somewhat of an unlucky mascot to several teams
during my playing days. In 1992, I played my last game for
Leeds United, which took them to the top of the table.
Manager Howard Wilkinson wanted to make sure they stayed
there – so he sold me to Luton the next day! Sure enough,
Leeds won the Championship – without me.

David Pleat, the Luton manager, signed me to change things.

Luton had been in the top division for ten years – the old First Division, now the Premiership. I certainly did help to change things – Luton were relegated!

I then went to my hometown club Middlesbrough, signing for Lennie Lawrence. It was their first season in the Premiership – 1992–93 – and even though Lennie had previously saved Charlton from going down for five years in the late 1980s and early 1990s, he reckoned without me! Middlesbrough went down!

Then there was the greatest escapologist since Harry Houdini – Dave 'Harry' Bassett, manager of Sheffield United. He was the manager who could get out of anything. But in the 1993–94 season he signed on that fateful unlucky mascot – you've probably guessed it by now – Sheffield United went down.

During this period struggling Coventry City were actually paying teams to sign me!

* * *

I am now enjoying a new career as football pundit, mainly for Sky. I can regularly be seen on the box commentating and reporting on matches, and also as a presenter alongside old favourites George Best, Rodney Marsh and Frank McLintock to name but a few. These chaps have actually nicknamed me God – 'God, he's on again!'

My old mate Gordon Strachan told me he thought his Sky dish had gone down when I didn't appear on his screen for one week!

I am kept so busy, my absence hasn't gone unnoticed at home. I recently returned home and my wife called out to my two sons, 'Dad's here!'

'Which channel?' came the reply.

FRANK KEATING

A Guardian sports columnist since the early 1970s, he has been named as the Sports Writer of the Year four times, the Sports Features Writer of the Year twice and in 1980, Columnist of the Year. Keating has written 15 books including biographies of Ian Botham and Graham Gooch, a history of rugby union and his own autobiography. He was an ITV Television producer between 1964 and 1972.

I have been writing daily waffle for *The Guardian* sports pages now for more than three decades. When I began, the sports desk was an unconsidered adjunct bereft of full-time staff and we would write by day and sub-edit the waffle ourselves into the pages at night. Helped no doubt by regular visits through an evening to the adjacent Blue Lion, we were all fairly punch-drunk by the last edition and I readily admit that I, probably more than anyone, was responsible for the papers affection-ately exasperated nicknames of the time: *the Grauniad, the Grundian* or *the Grungenad*. I can still recall a few of those famous misprints I let slip through, such as: 'A rash of no balls kept umpire Jones regularly gestating through the day.'

'Banks saved a certain goal when he died despairingly at Davies's feet.'

'Compared to Leeds's all-white strip, Chelsea took the eye with their irresistible passing and royal-blue skirts.'

'Uttley can play anywhere in the scrum – a typical England futility player …'

'A stony-faced Barrington last night accused Griffith of chuckling…'

'The quest for two pints has become the overriding factor in the inaugural season of the Welsh Heineken League'.

And one particular favourite: 'The last batsman, Albeit Carefully, survived till lunch.' Hooray for good ol' Albeit.

On a bad night I could even double them up, as in: 'The tall, blind, goalkeeper Bailey was discomfited in keeping out a rocket of a shit from Clark.'

One evening I dashed off some tribute to legendary cricketer, CB Fry, who had also been, in his prime, the world's long-jump record holder:

'In his Oxford rooms,' I wrote, 'one of the great man's party tricks to amuse fellow students was to jump backwards from carpet to mantelpiece from a standing start.'

Late that evening, I drifted back from the Blue Lion, perused the first edition, which had long 'gone', and read of Fry's ability to jump on the mantelpiece 'from a standing tart'. I changed it hastily for all further editions and staggered home. Next morning I checked the correction at breakfast – to learn, wouldn't you know, that Fry's party-piece was managed 'from a standing fart'.

" I like a boxer who quits in style."

SEAN KERLY

A Great Britain hockey player who played in the team which won the gold medal in the 1988 Olympics.

One of the most interesting places I have been was Darwin, in Australia's Northern Territory, where we landed on my first big trip abroad 20 years ago. We went out for a practice before playing against Northern Australia on a pitch that was bordered on three sides by a river. A ball was hit to me on the left wing, and I edged it towards the river.

I wandered through the vegetation near the river's edge when I saw this huge thing (which I thought was a log) slither into the water. I turned and sprinted back up to the pitch, scared out of my skin, without the ball, to be told that yes, it was an alligator, they live in the rivers around the coast.

That was the last ball I missed on that pitch!

* * *

I had a few embarrassing moments, actually many and varied – every time I went out to play. Probably the worst, though, was during the Olympics in 1984 in Los Angeles when I held up my team for many hours. Why? The team was waiting for me to produce a urine sample for a random drugs test after our losing semi-final against West Germany.

I had become so dehydrated during the game that it took me a *full four hours* to produce a sample – much to the consternation of all my team-mates!

An England rugby union international fly half who made his debut in June 1997 v Argentina. He has four caps to date.

Sean Connery has fallen on hard times. All work has dried up and he's just sat at home twiddling his thumbs.

Suddenly the phone rings and Sean answers it. It's his agent and Sean gets very excited.

The agent says, 'Sean, I've got a job for you. Starts tomorrow, but you've got to get there early, for 10-ish.'

Sean frowns and replies, 'Tennish? But I haven't even got a racket.'

JACK KYLE

An Ireland rugby union international, winning 46 caps, who helped Ireland to their only Grand Slam in 1948. He was also a Lions tourist in 1956.

A driver on a small road in the south of Ireland comes to a level crossing at a railway station which is half-way across the road. He sits in the car for ten minutes and then gets out and finds the station master and says, 'Do you know the gate is halfway across the road?'

'I do,' says the stationmaster. 'We are half expecting the train from Cork.'

* * *

Notice on the inside of the door of a small hotel in a remote part of Ireland:

'To call room service – open the door and call room service.'

L

MARK LAWRENSON

*A former Republic of Ireland international footballer, 'Lawro'
was capped 39 times by his country. He won many honours
with Liverpool, forming a legendary defensive partnership
with Alan Hansen. After hanging up his boots, he briefly
managed Oxford United and worked alongside Kevin Keegan
as a defensive coach at Newcastle. Lawrenson has been a
regular BBC football pundit since 1997, often teaming up
with old club-mate Hansen.*

Picture the scene – the 1986 FA Cup final, Liverpool beat
Everton 3–1 at Wembley and in doing so complete the Double.
They collect their medals and enjoy a lap of honour. On arriving
in the dressing room, it was time for a drink of bubbly out
of the famous Cup. Kit off, and into the bath to continue the
celebrations. However, the bath was already full – a number of
Liverpool fans had sneaked past the Wembley security and
were 'swimming', fully clothed, in our bath!!

* * *

My favourite joke:

A group of people are gathered at the Queen's garden party – as they are talking to Her Majesty, one of the gathering breaks wind! Immediately one of the Queen's aides says, 'How dare you fart before the Queen.'

To which he replies, 'I didn't know it was her turn!'

GRAEME LE SAUX

The former England defender signed for Chelsea in 1987, playing over 270 games for the club. He moved to Blackburn Rovers in 1993 where he lifted the Premiership title in 1995. His performances earned him a place in the England team where he won 36 caps after making his debut in 1994. He returned to Stamford Bridge in the summer of 1997.

A bear and a rabbit are in the woods, next to each other doing a poo. The bear says to the rabbit, 'Do you have a problem with poo sticking to your fur?'

The rabbit looks up at the bear and replies, 'No, of course not.'

So the bear picks up the rabbit and wipes his bottom with him!

FRANCIS LEE

A former England international footballer, he was a striker with Bolton Wanderers, Manchester City and Derby County and was chairman of Manchester City.

The new physio at Bolton Wanderers many years ago (we'll call him Bill) saw Mr Ted Gerrard alight from his Rolls Royce and limp across the car park into Burnden Park for a board meeting.

He noticed that Mr Gerrard was limping quite heavily so he strode over helpfully:

'Excuse me Mr Gerrard, but if you have time after the board meeting I will give you some DIATHERMIA on your leg.'

'Thee'll 'ave a job, lad', said Mr Gerrard, 'I lost it under a tram in Blackpool 30 years ago.'

Bill obviously didn't know that it was a wooden leg!!!

"This is an ambitious club, Battersby. We don't tolerate failure."

DONAL LENIHAN

An Ireland rugby union international, he captained his country and won 52 caps. A Lions tourist in 1983 and 1989, he was the Lions manager in 2001.

I was playing with my Irish partner, Moss Keane, for a Welsh invitation side in the south of France. Moss was idolised by the young Welsh hooker, who was fascinated by all the stories of Ireland's teak-tough second row. As often happened in France

167

at the time, a major fight erupted on the pitch. Everybody wades in, trading punches, except Moss who stands passively, arms folded. This shocked the Welsh no. 2. Later that night, fortified with several glasses of red wine, the young Welshman strikes up the courage to approach Moss.

'Moss,' he said, 'I've heard of your reputation as the hard man of Irish rugby. How come you didn't stand and fight today?'

'Look here,' Moss replied, 'whatever chance there is of me dying for Ireland, there is no f***ing way I am going to die for Wales.'

✳ ✳ ✳

France v Ireland, Parc des Princes 1982. Ireland have won the Triple Crown and Five Nations Championship and are playing for the Grand Slam. The team bus enters the stadium and is surrounded by French supporters who are going ballistic, thumping the windows and the side of the bus and shouting abuse at the team. The team is sitting in absolute silence – very tense. Not a word is being spoken. I am sitting next to Irish left wing Moss Finn. The French supporters are roaring, 'L'IRELANDE EST FINI – L'IRELANDE EST FINI.'

Moss Finn stands up.

'Christ, lads,' he says. 'Isn't it great to be recognised?'

JASON LEONARD

The most capped international rugby union international forward in the history of the game with 97 caps for England, he was a Lions tourist in 1997 and 2001.

A man is sitting at home quietly reading his newspaper when his wife sneaks up on him and whacks him around the head with a frying pan.

'What was that for?' he asks.

'That was for the piece of paper in your trouser pockets with the name Mary Ellen written on it,' she replies.

'Don't be silly,' he says. 'Two weeks ago when I went to the races, Mary Ellen was the name of one of the horses I bet on.'

She seems satisfied with this and apologises.

Three days later he's again sitting in his chair reading when she nails him with the frying pan, knocking him out cold.

When he comes round, he asks again:

'What was that for?'

She responds:

'Your f***ing horse phoned.'

JOSH LEWSEY

An England rugby union international, Lewsey made his debut in 1998 v New Zealand and in six appearances for his country has played at fly half, centre and full back.

This first story is one of fact! A certain current international player in his younger years first made fame by streaking at the annual Harrow v Eton cricket match at Lord's. As he hurdled the stumps, he knocked the bails off with his balls. The gentleman was immediately escorted from Lord's and was later banned from 'The Hill' for five years for degrading the school reputation.

Instead of regretting the incident, as the storm made national headlines – 'The boy in question was suspected to be an ex-pupil due to his physique,' he then boasted: 'Yeah, they said I was large!!'

* * *

The famous 72-year-old businessman, Lord Guinness, was on a chat show with the Ireland manager Brian O'Brian. The two studio guests were talking about how passionate rugby was. Lord Guinness the businessman said, 'I've earned millions of pounds, been to the most famous places in the world, I've got a beautiful wife and family. I've got everything. But what I would give to walk out at Lansdowne Road, down the tunnel in front of those people … well, I'd pay millions for that feeling.'

The Irish team manager, Brian O'Brian retorts, 'Well, if you give me one of those, sure you can play in the team!'

SEAN LINEEN

A Scotland rugby union international and a member of the 1990 Grand Slam-winning team, he played at centre and won 29 caps between 1989 and 1992.

When I first got the call-up to play for Scotland, I was flown up to Stornoway where my grandfather was born – this was the reason I could play for Scotland, being a New Zealander.

Before I left, Finlay Calder and John Jeffrey told me they speak only Gaelic on the island and they 'kindly' gave me some phrases to use.

On arriving at Stornoway I thought I would impress the media and island folk gathered at the airport by announcing in Gaelic what I thought meant: 'This is a lovely island and I am looking forward to meeting everyone.'

Well, they all had long faces and a few shakes of the head as I said,

'Pokemahone,' which basically means –'UP YOUR A**E!'

Never trust a forward …

GARY LINEKER

A former England footballer, he is the second highest goal scorer for his country with 48. Gary played for Leicester City, Everton, Barcelona, Tottenham Hotspur and Grampus Eight. He is now a BBC sports presenter.

When I was playing for Leicester, our manager, Gordon Milne, called a team meeting. He said we had received a police complaint saying that one of our players retaliated after being spat at by a Birmingham City supporter. Milne said, 'In the future if someone spits at you, you just have to swallow it.'

BILL LLENGICH

A broadcast journalist who has covered golf, cricket, rugby union and fishing.

I was in China, filming a feature on the Chinese rugby team. Now the sport was relatively new in the country – they may have a huge population but the team was very inexperienced and built around army regulars. We were invited by The People's Liberation Army to interview and film the team at practice. Never before had a TV crew managed to gain such an insight, it was a scoop to penetrate the complex security arrangements and notoriously secretive army headquarters.

The whisky makers – Famous Grouse – were sponsoring the team. They had flown Gavin Hastings out to coach them, and all was going superbly. We did our interviews, filmed all manner of sessions, and the relationship was excellent between ourselves and the Chinese army. Anything we requested, they obliged. Nothing was too much trouble.

As the final day was coming to an end, I wanted a final shot for the feature that would reflect all things good about the army, its rugby, the culture of the country and their progress. Near the pitch was a tatty old wall, with Chinese writing on it. Perfect, I thought, in the evening light I will get the players to stand in front of the wall, wearing their bright new international shirts, in wonderful contrast to the faded, crumbing wall behind them and get them to cheer.

I tried to explain this to the coach and his smiles turned to accusing stares, he stomped off. Maybe he misunderstood me, I thought, and talked to the captain of the team. Same result, if not a more aggressive response. Maybe they were just tired and fed up with being filmed. Persistent as always, I then went up to our interpreter and explained the situation. He looked at me aghast.

He told me the problem: 'You want the national team to stand in front of THAT wall, under THAT writing, and CHEER???'

'Yup,' I replied, now slightly nervous.

'That wall was the firing squad wall, and the writing translated means: 'all traitors of the People's Republic of China stand here and die.'

I haven't been invited back.

DAVID LLOYD

———— • ◆ • ————

A former England international cricketer with an average of 42, he has also coached his country. Nicknamed 'Bumble', he is now a television cricket analyst.

My son, Graham, scored his maiden first-class century and, naturally, I was very pleased and wanted to read all about this great feat in the press. So the next day, I promptly bought the newspaper. Imagine how I felt when I opened the paper, found the cricket section, and read: 'Graham Lloyd, son of the legendary, former West Indies captain Clive, scored his first maiden first-class century yesterday in The Parks ….'

* * *

Two Somerset lads went on *Stars in your Eyes*. They were wearing big sweaters with sheep on and declared that they were farmers.

Matthew Kelly said:

'And who are you going to be tonight, lads?'

(In Somerset accent) one replied:

'Tonight Matthew, we are going to be Simon and Garfunkel.'

'And what will you be singing for us?'

'Trouble over Bridgwater,' replied the other.

KENNY LOGAN

A Scotland rugby union international winger, he made his debut in 1992 and is the sixth most capped Scottish international of all time with 56 caps to date. Logan is also the third highest scorer in the history of the Scottish game.

There was a Scottish rugby fan watching a crucial Six Nations match in a pub in Edinburgh. Keeping him company was a row of whiskies and his faithful terrier Thistle. It was Scotland v England, the Grand Slam decider. England had possession, their big ugly pack rumbled towards the half-way line, then eventually gave the ball to the scrum half. He hoofed it upfield. Kenny Logan, playing on the wing, caught the ball. He began to run it back, but seeing a wall of Englishmen charging towards him, stopped, took aim and clipped over the most beautifully struck drop goal.

The Scotsman in the pub threw his arms in the air, Thistle

the dog jumped up on the bar, got up onto his hind legs, did a double back flip somersault, a quick breakdance routine and then slammed down two of the whiskies.

'Bloody hell, mate' said the barman. 'That's incredible, Logan only kicked a drop goal. What happens when Logan scores a try?'

'I dunno,' replied the Scotsman, 'I've only had him four years.'

"It's his great weakness. He can't stand the sight of blood—especially his own."

JONAH LOMU

The biggest box office draw rugby union has ever known, the 6'5", 248lb winger has won 58 caps for New Zealand, scoring 38 tries. He was the youngest All Black ever, making his debut aged 19 years and 45 days.

This has to be one of the classic tales about a Kiwi rugby player by the name of Glen Osborne, All Black full back in the 1995 World Cup and a man I have played alongside many times.

One day, Eric Rush, one of the all-time greats of All Black rugby, and I decided to bowl over to Glen's house. We sat down, had dinner with him and after our meal Glen jumps up and says he is going for a bath.

'Ah Yeh, we'll do the dishes,' we replied. So, we were running all the water but couldn't find the washing-up liquid anywhere. We walked into the bathroom to ask Glen and saw all these bubbles everywhere, all over the room, and Os (as he is known) was saying how much he was enjoying this bubble bath.

'Os, where is the Sunlight liquid?'

'Mate, it's here,' and he plucked it out from under all the bubbles.

'What is it doing in the bath?'

'Well I needed some bubbles for my bubble bath.'

What I have found is that Os does some really weird things.

We were getting ready for a Test match against France in 1995 and Os wanted to get some sleep during the day of the game. The doctor had said that you should only take a maximum of half a sleeping tablet. What does Os do? He drops two tablets. So, we had to carry him into the changing room in the lead-up to this huge match. He wakes up, and walks straight into the big mirror, thinking it was a door to another changing room.

We then went out to stretch and loosen off. We had one 'PowerAid' bottle with 'massage oil' written on it, while all the other bottles, for drinking, were bright red. Out of all the bottles available, Os picks up the massage oil and starts glugging. We were all watching and didn't know whether to laugh or cry.

How did he perform? Not only was he one of the most slippery players on show that night, but he caught the first high ball and scored a hat-trick, playing some of the best rugby we have ever seen.

*An England rugby union international winger, his presence
in international rugby is synonymous with tries. Luger is
currently England's third highest try scorer of all time with
19 tries in 27 appearances.*

I remember years ago I witnessed a scene that perfectly reflects how unique the game of rugby is, and typifies what the game is about. I was over in Ireland, and was watching a school match – the centre was tackled and a ruck formed. There was a scuffle at the bottom and a massive fight erupted. Both sides got stuck into each other.

This huge flanker grabbed the opposing scrum half by the shirt and pulled his fist back, ready to hit the little fella into next week. He had a massive fist cocked, when the whistle went for the end of the match.

Immediately the grimace turned to a smile, the fist unclenched and transformed itself into a warm handshake.

'Top game, thanks very much,' he said, and they walked away from the pitch chatting happily away.

Only in rugby …

* * *

There was once a man who had one great love in his life, his garden. Every day he used to wake up, draw the curtains, open the window and proudly look at his garden, smiling as he surveyed the view. The lawn was beautifully manicured, with an array of colour in a weed-less flowerbed; it was truly the perfect garden.

Well, one day he woke up, looked out of the window and to his horror saw a dirty great row of molehills, all over the lawn, in the flowerbeds, everywhere. He was distraught. He soon wiped his tears though, got out the *Yellow Pages* and found exactly what he was looking for.

'FOR THE BEST MOLE CATCHER IN TOWN, CALL KEITH WOOD – SIMPLY THE BEST.'

Well, this was in the days before Woody become a pro rugby player, and he regarded himself as simply the best. The distraught man rang him up and Woody said he would be round immediately.

So our hero set himself up in the garden, determined to catch the animal that had caused such a mess. He was up all night – no luck. The next morning he had to explain:

'Sorry mate, this is a very sneaky mole, but don't worry, I'll catch him.'

So Woody tried the second night – no luck.

'This has never happened before, this must be a champion mole, I admit I'm struggling a bit, certainly it's a tough task but I'll catch him.'

'Well, Mr Mole catcher,' replied the man, 'when you catch this damned mole, make him die the worst death you can imagine – really nasty.'

'No problem, Boss,' replied Woody, he was absolutely determined to put an end to this pest.

The next morning Woody strode into the man's house:

'I've caught him, just as I said I would!'

'Brilliant, and how did you kill him?'

'Horribly,' replied Woody, 'I buried him alive.'

DAN LYLE

A United States rugby union international, he has captained his country and won 32 caps to date.

As an initiative to increase bonding and do something a little different from the usual training routines, the management had organised for the Bath squad to go to do some training with 'The Commandos'. Our assignment – to run around The Citadel twice, in six teams, carrying a heavy log. Four men carrying, two resting but running alongside, all in rotation. Victor Ubogu was on my team, but in the relief two, not actually carrying the log. As we charged out of the gates we left most of the teams behind, and as it happened, Victor too. On our second lap, we were puffing, we were a team of five, not six, no Victor. We came to the finish line, the camera crews filmed the end, and noticed that we were one short.

Ten minutes later, up the hill trudges Victor. A camera crew rushes towards him and says:

'Victor, how is the team bonding going?'

Victor in reply:

'If I don't know these guys after ten years, this #*?!*ing won't help!'

SANDY LYLE

—————— •◆• ——————

A golf professional who has won two Majors, the 1985 Open Championship at Royal St George's and the 1998 Masters. He has also played in the Ryder Cup five times.

There I was playing at the Augusta National with Lee Trevino in a practice round for the 1988 Masters. Sometimes the weather can be awful but mostly we are treated with some hot April temperatures. This very day happened to be one of their glorious ones with the sun beating down on us nicely.

The course is always in immaculate condition, no weeds to be found anywhere and a fantastic display of colour from flowers out in bloom.

Absorbing and admiring our surroundings for the week, we also spotted a funny figure strolling along the fairways, wearing a hankie, with four knotted corners, as protective headwear.

Lee, having been to the British Isles many times, agreed it could only be a British tourist. The American's daily attire has included a baseball cap since the day they were invented. As we laughed and joked along the fairway, this person became more familiar to me. Could it be? Surely not! Oh yes, this person was my very own dear 'British' Dad.

Just by chance, did I not win that year?

He was a very proud Dad, even though we made him wear more suitable and less obvious headgear for the next four days.

MICHAEL LYNAGH

A former Australian rugby union international fly half, he is the Australian record points scorer with 911 and was part of Australia's World Cup-winning team in 1991. He is now a Sky TV analyst.

It was the early 1990s, just before a huge match against our old foes, New Zealand. Now there are times in the lead-up where you are flat-out training, and other times when there isn't much going on. Well, if you aren't up to much, the place where people generally tended to congregate was the physio's room. There were always players about, getting a rub or whatever. There we all were, the TV blaring away in the background, chatting away, when our second row, Garrick Morgan, walks in. We continued chatting away, and after a while Garrick speaks up.

'Who's that?' he says, pointing to the TV.

'That's Mikhail Gorbachev,' came the reply. Garrick remained silent for a couple of minutes, then: 'What does he do?'

'He's the head of the Soviet Union, one of the most powerful nations on earth.' We continued talking.

'What's that on his head?'

'Umm, it's a birthmark, mate.' Our conversation resumed. Finally Garrick responded, 'How long has he had it?'

* * *

Tim Horan and me have been close mates a long time, we've played rugby together for years and go back a long way. Back in 1992, Tim came to stay with me and my wife in Treviso, Italy. We were keen to show Tim a good time, and so organised a trip to what is regarded as one of the most stunning cities in the world – Venice. First impressions last, as they say. Tim took one look at the famous old city and said,

'Bloody hell, it's been raining a lot here mate, all the roads are flooded.'

'No Tim, this is what Venice is like, it's made up of canals, that's how you get about, all by water.'

'But mate, where do all the cars go?'

* * *

We had just flown into the airport from abroad and the whole squad of us had disembarked and were waiting in the baggage hall, by the carousel. Bags were going around and around, we were waiting for ours patiently when something caught our eye. Striding across towards our carousel was a drugs squad officer with a sniffer dog in tow. He let the dog off the lead and it ran to the carousel and bounded onto the bags, rummaging around.

Jason Little saw all this:

'Isn't that great,' he said.

'What's so great, Jason?' came the reply.

'Well, isn't it great, the dog is looking for the blind man's luggage.'

Lysaght is the BBC Radio 5 Live racing correspondent,
appointed in July 2001.

A diminutive flat jockey friend, Martin Dwyer, was driving to the races when he was confronted by a flood stretching on the road in front of him for as far as the eye could see.

Despite the obvious perils, Dwyer boldly pressed on, egged on by his passenger, another jockey, called Steve Drowne, until, with the water becoming deeper and deeper, the car spluttered to a halt, as ignominious as it was inevitable.

Opening the doors was completely out of the question, so, able (for once) to take advantage of their size, the pair clambered out through their respective windows, before discarding their shoes and socks on the roof, and attempted to push the vehicle from trouble.

Unsurprisingly, such a course of action did not prove terrifically successful, not least because the torrent was reaching new depths, making size an issue once again. However, a four-wheel drive Good Samaritan appeared around the corner just as the going was getting impossibly heavy, and towed them away to dry land.

All, then, was ultimately well, but there was a moral to the story. I said to Dwyer, 'Call me an old fool, but perhaps it was not the brightest idea in the world to indulge in aquatic adventures with only a chum named Drowne for assistance.'

* * *

The image of the jump jockey, especially the brave bunch from Ireland, is one of endearingly brainless courage, otherwise why on earth would they do it? Although the notable exploits of several Irish-born riders have gone some considerable way towards rubbishing this 'T'ick Mick' caricature, there are, of course, exceptions to all rules.

One rang Weatherby's, the racing administrators at Wellingborough, on his birthday. Let's say, for argument's sake, that it was the 1st March – to check the balance on his account. Asked for his date of birth as a security check, he replied:

'It's the first of the third in such-and-such a year.'

The clerk at the other end of the line, a friendly soul, wished him Happy Birthday.

Bemused at her knowledge, our perplexed hero inquired:

'How did yer know?'

M

ROD MacQUEEN

MacQueen was coach of the Australian team that won the 1999 rugby union World Cup.

It was just before the first test against the British and Irish Lions in 2001. Our training had gone well and I had sat down with my other coaches and we had chosen the team. I always like to ring each player to either congratulate them on selection, or take the time to explain why they had not made the side.

I was driving from Sydney to Canberra and I was calling the players during the long trip to tell them the news. The phone was on speaker for ease of driving, with my wife in the passenger seat.

'Hello, so and so, it's Rod MacQueen, congratulations, you are in the team.'

'Thanks very much, Rod,' and so it went on.

Myself and my wife, who could of course hear the conversations, took great pleasure in hearing the delight from the players when they heard the news.

Next on the list was George Smith, the hugely talented young openside who had not played much international rugby. This was a huge Test series against the Lions and it meant so much to all selected.

'Hi, George, it's Rod MacQueen.'

'Yeh, sure, piss off.'

'No George, seriously, it's Rod MacQueen. Congratulations you are in the team.'

'What a load of b***ocks, sure you are Rod MacQueen.'

'Well George, if you don't believe me, ring another member of the management team and check.'

I put the phone down, looked and laughed with my wife who could hear the whole thing on speaker. Five minutes later, the phone rang ….

'Mr MacQueen, it's George Smith here, I'm SO, SO sorry ….'

His mates had obviously been winding him up previously! And I thought George Smith was always such a polite young man!

∗ ∗ ∗

I always thought it was wonderful that when we went on tour with the Wallabies, we always managed to go off and have a game of golf. I always appreciated that, during the times that the player/coach relationships weren't always that good, the players would still come up and ask me for a game.

At last I realised why. When they came on tour they never brought much spending money and whenever the boys were short of cash they asked me for a game of golf. I of course, ended up paying the green fees. They called me the ATM machine – Automatic Teller MacQueen.

RODNEY MARSH

A former England international footballer, who played for QPR,
Manchester City and Fulham, and is now a Sky TV analyst.

I was capped nine times for England and I'm often asked why I only got nine. Well, here's the reason why:

England were playing Northern Ireland in the Home Nations Championships and they were tough opposition in those days with the likes of George Best and Pat Jennings in their line-up. Alf Ramsey was England manager at the time, a cockney like me, but he had taken elocution lessons before the World Cup finals in 1966 so now he spoke very posh.

Before the game Alf gave his team talk and stressed that if we were to win the game we would have 'to work very hard'.

He went on:

'As a team we must work harder, you in particular Rodney. You must work harder when you play for England. I've told you before when you play for England you can't play the way you usually do. In fact, this is your last chance. If you don't work harder tonight I will pull you off at half-time.'

'That's brilliant,' I said. 'At Man City we only get a cup of tea and an orange!'

Funnily enough, that was the last time I ever played for England!

＊　＊　＊

Malcolm Allison, Francis [Franny] Lee and myself went to the Brooke House Hotel in Wilmslow Road, just around the corner from the Man City ground. We used to call it the club hotel.

The guy who owned it was called Jim Barker. I'll never forget him. He was a super man and a City fanatic. When we got to the bar, Malcolm immediately ordered Bollinger and we spent the afternoon telling jokes and generally having a good time.

After a few more bottles of champagne we had a little party going. When it got to about 2 p.m. and our sixth or seventh bottle, I phoned my wife Jean and warned her that I was going to be a bit late.

We carried on drinking all afternoon until we had emptied a staggering 23 bottles of champagne. Finally Malcolm surveyed the one remaining bottle from the two cases that were still on the bar and called Jim over.

'Jim,' he slurred, 'no more. I'm not going to have the 24th bottle. I don't want people to think I'm a flash bastard!'

And with that he wrote out a cheque for the damage and staggered through the door! Despite the amount we had drunk, when we got outside into the hotel grounds Franny climbed into his brand new lime green Mercedes, his prize possession, a car he had collected just days before. Thankfully, before he got out of the car park he drove it straight into the back of a Triumph Herald and had to get a taxi instead!

TOMMY MARTYN

———————— •◆• ————————

The St Helens half back has scored over 1,000 points, including over 150 tries in a career that started at Oldham where he played between 1989 and 1993. He then moved to St Helens where he won the Challenge Cup in 1997, scoring two tries to beat Bradford. He has played over 200 games for the club, has 8 caps for Ireland and 4 caps for Great Britain.

We were drawn to play Oldham away in this year's Challenge Cup. For various reasons the game was switched to a neutral venue and Stalybridge Celtic's football ground was chosen.

When told we were off to Stalybridge Celtic to play, Sean Hoppe asked, 'Why do we have to play in Scotland?'

* * *

Our coach, Ian Millward, decided to freshen us up by changing our training schedule one week. He announced that the next day, instead of working at the training ground, we would be going to a local paintball centre to play Skirmish. Full back Paul Wellens asked in all innocence:

'Who are Skirmish? I've never even heard of them.'

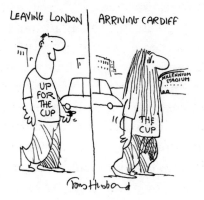

JASON McATEER

He has won more than 50 caps for the Republic of Ireland and was in Mick McCarthy's squad for the 2002 World Cup finals in Japan and Korea. The defender captained his country on his 50th appearance and has played in two World Cups. He has played for Bolton, Liverpool and Blackburn Rovers and now plays for Sunderland.

My Ireland colleague Mark Kennedy walked into a Pizza Hut one Saturday night. When the pizza was ready, he was asked:

'Sir, would you like your pizza cut into four or eight slices?'

'Please cut it into four,' he replied. 'I could never eat eight.'

JOHN McCRIRICK

Channel 4 Racing presenter and one of the most eccentric and loved characters in racing. He started work as a private handicapper before working for the Sporting Life *from 1972 until 1983. He was named Specialist Writer of the Year in 1978, Campaigning Journalist of the Year in 1979, and Sports Presenter of the Year in 1992.*

'There, on the favourite, is the unmistakeable Kieren Fallon – or is it Frankie Dettori?'

Unnamed Channel 4 commentator – he's paid me to keep his anonymity.

* * *

Princess Anne was riding in an amateur riders event at Epsom and just as I was about to give a shriek from the betting ring, I heard a desperate appeal from my producer down my earpiece, 'For goodness sake, John, don't say the bookies want to lay Princess Anne!'

It never entered my mind ... on the other hand ...

GLEN McCRORY

A former world Cruiserweight champion and sparring partner of Mike Tyson, McCrory is now a Sky TV presenter and commentator.

I was picked to go over to spar with Mike Tyson in 1997 when he was the most feared man on the planet; his camp had offered me a trial, on $200 a week. A flight and 32 hours on a national bus later I arrived, only to find someone had nicked my suitcase on the journey.

Well, I couldn't tell the camp that some sneak thief had

dared to steal Tyson's sparring partner's bag, I would have been laughed out the door all the way back home. All I had was my gloves, headguard and the jeans and jacket I was wearing.

At the time James Tillers and Oliver McCall were in sparring as well. An awesome set-up. I was introduced to the mean machine and I said I was ready and hungry to spar, too nervous to mention I had no kit.

One problem – no kit.

So I sneaked out to the local Army and Navy store, and only having 30 bucks in my pocket, I bought what I could. The next day, facing the baddest man on the planet, was me, in white ten-dollar plimsoles, little shorts and a white string vest, three sizes too small. I lasted four rounds, longer than any of the other sparring partners. Not because I could match him, but because he was too busy laughing.

BRIAN McDERMOTT

A prop forward who has played over 250 games for the Bradford Bulls, he won a Championship-winners medal in 2000 and lifted the Challenge Cup the same year, when Bradford beat Leeds in the final at Murrayfield. McDermott has won 4 caps for Great Britain and 1 for England.

Our prop forward, Stuart Fielden, is always moaning about his pay packet and all the deductions for tax, etc. On one occasion he was complaining about paying tax and how much he'd lost in National Insurance and said: 'The one thing that really winds me up is the amount I have to pay to this Miss Cellaneous every week. Who is she?'

It was eventually explained to him that she was actually … miscellaneous!

A former Scotland international footballer, he also played for Aston Villa, Celtic and Bayern Munich. He is now a television analyst.

It's 1990, the World Cup in Italy and our first game was against Costa Rica, we were heavy favourites to win the game but the manager of the time – Andy Roxborough, couldn't decide who he was going to put up front. In the squad were myself, Ally McCoist, Maurice [Mo] Johnson and Robert Fleck. One, two or even three up front, we had no idea. The boss eventually started talking about the tactics, and used pieces of paper to show who he wanted where.

'Mo and Nally, you are the men up front,' he said at last.

Now Ally McCoist, who I was rooming with, thought he said 'Ally', not 'Nally', which was my nickname. He was well chuffed with himself, thinking he was going to play; we all, though, realised that he meant me. As the chat continued, Roxborough kept looking at me directly: 'Look big man, I want you to this, I want you to that …' and we could all see Ally physically deflate. So he took a big breath and 'accidentally' exhaled very swiftly. All the paper men flew everywhere, Roxborough's tactics were ruined.

Anyway, I was chuffed to bits and after this evening session I went off for a rub, and when I got back to my room there was Ally, pissed off, lying in bed. He was reading the paper, doing the crossword. I turned on the TV, but my Italian is not the best and there were no porn channels, so I switched it off.

He had his light on, on his side of the room.

'Coisty,' I said.

'Yeh, big man' he replied.

'Turn that light off, some of us have got a game tomorrow!'

He was really cheesed off. We played the game the following day, we got beaten 1–0 and everyone was on a downer.

The next game was against Sweden, but I had hurt my calf, so was out. I was bitterly disappointed this time. Coisty was still not picked to play. Maurice Johnson and Robert Fleck were the men up front. He was suicidal. We both had to get our heads up.

After lunch, I was lying on my bed, Coisty bounces in, with a newspaper in each hand. He strides over to me and says, 'Right big man, you can help me do the crossword this time!'

DUNCAN McKENZIE

A former England international footballer, he has also played for Nottingham Forest, Leeds, Anderlecht and Everton and Chelsea.

In 1975, I was warming up as a sub for Leeds v Carlisle, and wearing canvas jogging bottoms and roll-neck sweater, I was mistaken by a police officer for a pitch invader.

He promptly put his arm round my neck and twisted my arm up my back and frogmarched me towards the exit. Approximately 40,000 witnesses aided my release – his face was even redder than mine.

* * *

In 1977 while still playing for Everton, I was asked to make a speech at Tranmere Rovers. A Question and Answer session ensued. Despite a few pleas from myself, questions were still infrequent.

A blind Liverpool fan sat at the back and shouted out, 'Get off, you bluenose.'

Thirty seconds of silence later, he shouted again, 'Has he gone?'

BILL McLAREN

*Known as 'The voice of Rugby', he commentated on his last
game for the BBC in the 2001–2002 Six Nations
championship. He saw a 27–22 victory by his beloved
Scotland over Wales at the Millennium Stadium after 50
years behind the microphone.*

Rikki Fulton, the Scottish comedian, was giving his impression
of an inebriated weatherman, and informed his listeners/TV
viewers that, 'There are an awful lot of isobars about – and I've
been in every one of them.'

* * *

Jim Renwick, capped 52 times by Scotland at Rugby Union,
pulled the leg of his national team colleague, Bruce Hay, who
was never liable to break the sound barrier, that once, when
Bruce thundered up the wing, it was the first time he had seen
a player flat out and in slow motion at one and the same time!

GORDON McQUEEN

*A former Scotland international footballer, McQueen was
signed by Don Revie from St Mirren to Leeds in 1972 for
the modest fee of £30,000. He went on to make 170 first
team appearances, scoring 19 goals. The defender had spells
of coaching and managing St Mirren and Aidrie and four
years as a co-commentator on Scottish television. He is now
in charge of the reserves at Middlesbrough.*

I was playing for Leeds United under the very strict and
demanding Don Revie. I suffered concussion and approached
the touchline to inform 'the Boss'.

'I can see two balls and cannot continue.'
To which he replied:
'Get back on the pitch and kick both.'

* * *

When I was manager of Airdrie in Scotland, I reported to the board at our weekly meeting that one of our players had suffered a 'detached retina'. The clueless Chairman demanded to know what was happening at training, as this was the third knee injury that month!

STAN MELLOR

Three times Champion National Hunt jockey and the first National Hunt jockey to ride 1,000 winners.

Mr Albert Jones, an amateur rider, had a ride in the three-mile chase at Leicester. On his return a rather officious Clerk of the Scales asked him if he had completed the course.

'Yes Sir,' replied Albert and, with a big grin on his face, walked into the dressing room.

Some time later the Clerk of the Scales learned that Mr Jones's horse had actually fallen. Annoyed with Mr Jones, he went briskly into the dressing room to have a word.

'You told me that you had completed the course. I have now been told that your horse fell,' he accused.

'I did complete, Sir,' said Mr Jones, still smiling. 'I set off into the race with two circuits to go. I went once around on the horse and once round in the ambulance.'

* * *

'You give them the winners,' I was told by my host in the private box at Cheltenham. Present were ten business clients, myself and the host, who was a very experienced racing man. Realising why I had been invited, I duly went though the card with some suggestions.

There was a horse in the first race that had been unlucky in his previous run, which I told them would run well and be good value at 7/1. He made all the running but was just caught on the line. Most racing people would have considered that they'd had a good run at good value, but to the guests in the box, he was just a loser.

'What will win the next?' they asked with a little less enthusiasm. I said it was an open race; any one of them could win, but advised them not to back the favourite. In his previous race he had not looked genuine and he would not relish the uphill finish at Cheltenham.

Ten minutes later the favourite stormed up, winning by eight lengths! My host, dismayed by the wilting morale of his guests, approached me:

'Mellor,' he said, 'I always suspected you couldn't tip a winner, but now I know you can't tip a loser either!'

NIGEL MELVILLE

—————————— • ◆ • ——————————

A former England rugby union international captain, he won 13 caps between 1984 and 1988. He is a former Wasps Director of Rugby and is now the Director of Rugby at Gloucester.

Rob Henderson returned to training at London Wasps having played well for Ireland versus South Africa at the weekend.

As I was his coach, we discussed the finer points of his performance, particularly the fact he had made a 40 m break but was caught just in front of the try line. His reason?

'I was weighed down,' he said.

'But I thought you had been training well and lost weight,' I replied.

'I have,' he said, 'but I nipped out for a cigarette just before kick-off and left my lighter in my shorts pocket.'

Rob had played the whole first half with his cigarette lighter in his pocket. He realised it was there when both teams lined up for kick-off, but it would have been too embarrassing to hand his lighter to someone on the touch line!

KATHARINE MERRY

Katharine is the top ranked 400m runner in Britain and ran a fantastic personal best of 49.72 to win the bronze medal behind Lorraine Graham and Cathy Freeman at the 2000 Sydney Olympics.

My Olympic medal broke and they wanted to replace it with another one. I said no as it was the one I received on the rostrum. They said I had to. I said no! In the end I left Sydney with two Olympic bronze medals! Quite a result.

I have one and my parents have the original in their house. I think it's the easiest Olympic medal ever gained!

DIANE MODAHL

The 1990 Commonwealth 800m champion and six times British champion.

At the 1993 World Athletic Championships in Stuttgart I was in top form, mentally prepared for the inevitable pressures and physically at the peak of my form; I was convinced all would go well. During the first of three rounds I could feel a slight unease under my foot when I put my spikes on. Ignoring it and progressing into the semi final the next day, I was still plagued by an uneasy feeling in the shoe of my left spike.

The next day was the final – after completing it and finishing just outside the medals, I realised (once the shoes had come off) that the unease I could feel in my shoe – was a folded piece of paper: a love letter from my husband!

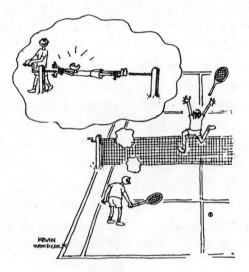

DEWI MORRIS

A former England rugby union international scrum half, winning 26 caps, he helped England to the Grand Slam in 1992 and was a Lions tourist to New Zealand in 1993. He is now a television analyst.

I had been reappointed scrum half for the France v England match in Paris in 1994 after Kyran Bracken had been dropped after the defeat at the hands of Ireland two weeks earlier. It was a huge selection battle between us and I was pumped up to the eyeballs. Parc des Princes waited, beautiful sunshine, but with the French smelling the blood of Englishmen. We had not lost to the French for six years and they were steaming.

The game was brutal, tough physical confrontations from the first whistle. We had the ideal game plan, keep the discipline, kick the penalties, Brian Moore to wind the hell out of the opposition – leave in one piece, victorious!

Well, this was going to plan, the French were getting wound up, constantly killing the ball, we were kicking the penalties. However I was also getting very wound up, as try-scoring opportunities were going begging – due to the French killing the ball.

Half-way through the second half, I had had enough. Another ruck, the ball was just about to appear when the French hands again appeared. I snapped. I straightened up, took a pace towards the ref and shouted at the ref in my limited French vocabulary:

'MONSIEUR, MONSIEUR, LE BALLON, LE BALLON, LE FRANCAIS NON RELEASEE, S'IL VOUS PLAIT MONSIEUR?'

At which point Stephen Hilditch turned to me and said in his beautiful Irish lilt:

'It's OK Dewi, I can understand English.'

JOHN MOTSON

———— •◆• ————

John Motson has been a member of the Match of the Day team for 30 years and is regarded by many as the BBC's voice of football. He has commentated on over 1,000 matches for the BBC including FA Cup, European Championship and World Cup finals.

I once said during a *Match of the Day* commentary:
'For the benefit of those watching in black and white, Spurs are in the yellow shirts.'

* * *

When Gary Lineker scored a hat-trick for Everton on the last day of the 1985–86 season, I said in my report, 'Lineker has now scored 39 goals this season – exactly TWICE as many as he got last year.'

I still don't know how Gary managed to get 19½ the year before!

SCOTT MURRAY

———————— • ◆ • ————————

A Scotland rugby union international with 40 caps to date, the athletic second row was a Lions tourist in 2001.

It was during the World Cup 1999 – there is quite a lot of time off and you tend to get pretty bored. It so happened that Tom Smith, myself and Martin Leslie were all together. At the time Reebok had a huge campaign going across the country, using various players who were playing. In Wales there were huge posters of Rob Howley around: 'ROB HOWLEY WEARS REEBOK, HOWLEY THE WHIRLWIND.'

Our very own Scottish hero Gregor Townsend had his catch line: 'GREGOR TOWNSEND WEARS REEBOK, TOWNSEND THE TIMEBOMB.'

So every time we went out we used to take the Mickey and put up little A4 posters in restaurants, in Post Office windows, etc: 'GREGOR TOWNSEND WEARS SUSPENDERS, TOWNSEND THE CROSS DRESSER.'

He was hating it ….

The three of us were particularly bored one day, and we acquired four big A3 sheets of paper from the tactics flip chart and composed the biggest and most impressive ad campaign for Gregor yet.

We stole the buggy kart, zipped up to the end of the road and sellotaped this poster to the side of the bus stop.

It had been two weeks of constant banter and he was getting pretty wound up.

Soon afterwards we all jumped onto our bus to go to another training session, and drove towards the bus stop with the poster. There, covering the whole of the bus stop was the ad campaign – displaying Gregor's talents for all to see: 'GREGOR TOWNSEND WEARS SUSPENDERS, TOWNSEND THE CROSS DRESSER.'

He sprinted up to the front of the bus, screams to the driver to stop, jumps out and tears it down. All the boys were pissing themselves laughing.

At last Gregor turns shy. He rips down – his pin up!

N

PHIL NEAL

An England football international, winning 50 caps, he played for Liverpool, winning eight championships, four League Cups, four European Cups and one UEFA Cup.

I was approached by a 'lady of the night' in O'Connell Street in Dublin. She said:

'Would you like to sleep with me for a fiver?'

My reply: 'I'm not very tired but the money will come in handy.'

O

MARTIN OFFIAH

The most deadly English rugby league try scorer in the history of the game, he scored over 500 career league tries, has played international rugby league for Great Britain, and club rugby for Widnes, Wigan, London Broncos and Salford. He now plays rugby union for Wasps.

Myself and Lennox Lewis went to a Snoop Doggy Dog Concert not so long ago. I've been mistaken for other people loads of times – Ian Wright, Ellery Hanley to name but two, but I thought if there is one man that is instantly recognisable it is the great man Lennox, he's famous – worldwide. So I did laugh when we arrived at the entrance and the security guard said:

'This way Martin, and Saracen.'

I was grinning widely. Lennox, on the other hand, chose not to hear that he'd been mistaken for a Gladiator.

* * *

While doing a fashion show for a friend and top designer, William Hunt, I was given some fake rings to wear as accessories. I decided to liven the show up a bit more. I walked to the end of the catwalk and threw the rings into the audience. Dwight Yorke was right behind me, strutting his stuff too. He decided to do the same thing, but ended up catapulting his platinum engraved *real* ring with his fake ones by mistake.

He blamed me until after the show, when we went to look for it. There it was, untouched on the floor. The audience obviously saw it and decided it was a fake so left it!

Alas I couldn't find my fake rings anywhere ...

JOHN OLVER

A former England rugby union international hooker, he won three caps between 1990 and 1992.

While the England team were staying in Edinburgh for the Scotland match, I was sharing a room with Dean Richards. One of our scams was to take all our dirty washing and dry cleaning with us that could be weeks old, and get it laundered at the hotel on the RFU account. One player even took his curtains down and got them dry-cleaned at the RFU's expense. The hotel was a very sophisticated one, and when our clothing returned, the shirts were in individual boxes with the hotel crest on them. I was going through them, giving Dean his and keeping mine, when the Orrell prop Martin Hynes, who was a replacement, came in, looked and said:

'Where did you get those new shirts from?'

I turned to Dean, smiled and replied:

'If you can keep a secret, we'll tell you.'

Martin said he could, so I told him that we knew the head porter very well, we were measured for the shirts yesterday in Princes Street and that the head porter charged the shirts to the RFU's hotel sundries bill. No one would ever know. Martin asked if he could be included but we said it was too late;

however, we had a similar arrangement in London at the Petersham Hotel in Richmond and we were getting suits made next time, again at the RFU's expense. We magnanimously added that we could include a couple of shirts for Martin.

I briefed the hotel staff in London and when the next international weekend came around, the trap was set. Martin phoned through his measurements and was looking forward to receiving his new shirts. I had also briefed the England manager Geoff Cooke. Geoff stood up at a team meeting and said he had discovered people ordering shirts on the RFU's bill and would they own up. There was complete silence and Martin looked over at Dean and myself for some guidance. We both totally ignored him, he was getting very hot under the collar.

After some more questioning from Geoff, Simon Halliday stood up and pointed at me, saying that I was the likely culprit as I was always doing these things (what a good bloke!).

Eventually Martin took a big gulp and announced that he had ordered the shirts but he then added that Dean Richards and John Olver had ordered suits!! He had grassed us up!

The few that were in on the set-up, like Will Carling, Peter Winterbottom and Geoff Cooke, just exploded with laughter.

When the rest of the squad realised the wind-up, and that Martin had reported us two as well, he did take a bit of stick!

"We think you Aussies are the best side ever."

A former Ireland international rugby union full back and
captain, winning 35 caps. He has played club rugby for
London Irish and Leinster and was the Allied Dunbar
Premiership Player's Player of the Year 1998–99. He is now
Director of Rugby at London Irish.

Justin Bishop, the London Irish and Ireland wing, was celebrating his first cap and try-scoring debut v South Africa. There he was in the bar enjoying his beers. Now, Justin isn't your typical Irishman, more the East Grinstead Geezer, a Londoner through and through. He is qualified to play for Ireland, for the record, due to Irish parents.

Anyway, deep into the evening our hero was approached by a supporter with a very strong Irish accent. This fan congratulated Bishop heartily on his successful debut, to which Bishop replied:

'Sorry mate, I don't speak Afrikaans.'

So much for the Irish knowing their own.

* * *

Gary Halpin, the London Irish and Ireland prop was playing against Leicester in the Cup semi-final at Sunbury. The game was in full flow when the tannoy announcer made a call to the crowd:

'Could the owner of car Reg. no T235 OUN please move their car …'

As the scrum formed, Halpin took stock, stood up and ran to the sideline to admit that it was his car was the one blocking the ambulance.

The game was held up for five minutes as Halpin got his keys.

P

ERIC PETERS

*A Scotland rugby union international flanker who has won
29 caps to date, he made his debut in 1995 v Canada and
has lately bravely beaten cancer to return to the top level of
the game.*

Clive Woodward was assistant coach at Bath before taking on
the England job in the autumn of 1997. At a Monday meeting
after Jack Rowell had resigned from England, the press were
speculating about Clive as his replacement. Clive assured us
he'd be with Bath until the end of the season.

He then came in on the Tuesday to say he was leaving Bath
to coach England with immediate effect, to which Richard
Webster piped up:

"Oh, I get it Clive. So you will be coaching us to the end of
the strawberry season then?"

He had no answer but fair play, he just laughed along.

* * *

On the field, playing alongside Henry Paul, for Bath against
Llanelli in 1996.

He played full back for the first time. He caught a kick in his own in-goal and in rugby league you don't want to get caught there, so he ran it out. Then he realised he could touch it down in Union, so ran back into his in-goal, then realised he couldn't now touch it down or it would be a five-yard scrum to the opposition. So, he ran out again and was wasted by eight Llanelli players chasing up the kick. Teething problems of changing codes ...

AGUSTIN PICHOT

The most capped Argentinian rugby union scrum half of all time with 43 caps. He was Argentina's Sports Personality of the Year in 1999.

We were on tour to France back in 1992. We were a young team and a bit strapped for cash. We had some fantastic experiences and saw many new sights, but one we turned into our advantage.

As we wandered around the sights of the great city of Paris, we saw some buskers. All sorts of actors, comedians and musicians were trying to carve out a living around the capital.

Anything they could do, so could we ...

So, a group of us picked ourselves a tactical spot right under the Eiffel Tower, a perfect position. Now all we had to do was create something worth a franc or two.

One grabbed a guitar and started strumming away furiously, the rest of us, with no instrument to hand, started singing, and dancing around. We persevered, and gave it all we had for many hours, looking forward to picking up some tidy pocket money at the end of the day. We certainly drew crowds, curious to know what on earth this group of crazy Argentinians were up to.

'Can somebody get me out of this bloody suit?!'

Only mad dogs and Englishmen go up against Merv Hughes.

Going, going, gone …

Robin needed extra
cash, but a paper round
was out of the question.

Tuffers prepares for a long spell in the field.

John celebrates winning the court case against his tailor.

Vinnie denies rumours of a Jane Fonda affair.

Things didn't go so well for Ray after the other players started wearing garlic.

20 a day – birdies that is.

God arrest ye merry gentlemen.

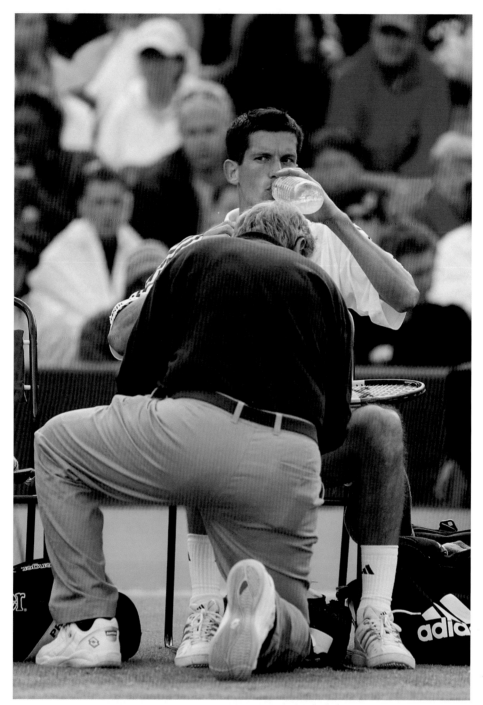

'There is definitely some swelling, as for your knee … '

Niall had seen *The Karate Kid* one too many times for McCarthy's liking.

'You might run fast mate but we both know who'd cross the line first in a dead heat.'

'What do you mean we're in?!'

At last, exhausted, we packed up. The moment had come – how much had we made? A hundred, two hundred francs even?

Ten francs!

The financial rewards were poor, but the laugh we had was priceless!

LESTER PIGGOTT

He rode his first winner at the age of 12 in 1948, was a champion jockey in England 11 times and won the Derby a record nine times between 1954 and 1983. He retired in 1995 aged 59.

Among the many great jockeys Australia has provided are George Moore and Roy Higgins. On a visit to Sydney I had been invited to spend the day with trainer Bart Cummings on his boat.

The Yacht Club was deserted and I couldn't find which way to go. Seeing a door marked 'Secretary', I knocked. The woman who opened the door stood and stared at me. Before I had a chance to say a word, she shrieked, 'I know you, you're George Piggins!'

There's simply no answer to that!!

* * *

I have always loved ice-cream. A favourite stop was 'Baskin-Robbins' on the Finchley Road, and I often called by on the way out of London. A new girl was behind the counter one evening. As she handed me my cone, she uttered the immortal words, 'Are you Wilson Pickett?'

RICHARD PITMAN

A former steeplechase jockey best known for losing the
Grand National and Cheltenham Gold Cup within a three-
week period in 1973. Pitman is a widely-respected BBC
racing commentator and analyst, a former husband of
trainer Jenny Pitman and father of trainer Mark Pitman.

Driving to 'The Maze' racecourse in Northern Ireland at night for a speaking engagement, we were stopped in a back lane by a lone soldier with blackened face, machine gun and a searchlight on his head.

He asked to search the car and he felt through my suitcase until he put his hand on my wig that was in the washbag. His reaction? He screamed in shock, threw it up in the air and immediately another dozen soldiers hiding in a ditch on either side of the road switched on their searchlights and trained their guns on my hairpiece which was now lying majestically in the middle of the road, bathed in a pool of light!

Imagine me having to walk into the lights to retrieve my hair, and the ribbing the first soldier took from the squad.

* * *

1978, Lord Oaksey and I rode around the Aintree Grand National course for BBC TV. He wanted us to miss the third fence as it has a 6′6″ open ditch in front and thought horses might refuse to jump it in cold blood.

We galloped and jumped the first two fences and then rode at the third, only to pull up sharply just before take-off. We then went around to the landing side and backed up to the fence, gave the horses a kick and set off.

'With good editing, no one will spot the difference,' he reasoned. We completed the course and it made a superb feature for 'Grandstand'.

The next year I repeated the stunt with Captain Mark Phillips, who was riding the Queen's grey eventer, Columbus, and told him Oaksey's plan from the year before.

'Rubbish' he said; he wanted to jump all the fences.

I rode Baroney Fort who had refused the year before in the Grand National itself. Up came the third fence. Sure enough, he stopped and ejected me.

There I was, lying on the turf, winded, only to roll over to see Lord Oaksey laughing.

'Richard,' he said, 'it's no good getting older, if you don't get wiser.'

Mark and I both finished the course, eventually.

PAT POCOCK

An England international cricketer between 1967 and 1985, he played 25 Test matches, bowling right arm off breaks. His best figures were 6–79.

As a young professional at 18, I was playing a benefit match at Aldermaston on the hottest day of the year (about 90 degrees). To show how long ago it was I was, asked to open the batting with Stuart Surridge. After batting for an hour or so, scoring about 30 runs, I came off dripping wet with sweat and soaked through.

In the dressing room was Ron Tindall [Tinners]. Ron played cricket for Surrey and football for Chelsea.

'Where are the showers?' I asked.

Ron said, 'There aren't any.'

'Oh no,' I said, and Ron's reply?

'Don't worry, they have made arrangements for us to have a shower over there.' He pointed me in the direction of a rather grand house.

He told me not to go to the front door but I would find a door around the back and first on the left was the shower room. I took up my wash bag with all the powder and smellies, went in the door and sure enough on the left was a bathroom. There was no shower so I ran a nice bath. After a few minutes I was singing away and a man came in and his mouth dropped.

'I was told I could have a shower over here – couldn't find one so had a bath instead.'

'Eh, Eh, Eh, OK' he said and went out.

I went back to the dressing room, cool as a mountain stream, and Tinners said, 'Where have you been?'

'I couldn't find a shower so I had a bath instead – lovely.'

Ron then replied, 'You plonker – I was only joking!'

'Plonker or not pal, I am going to be the only one who gets a bath.'

RICHARD POOL-JONES

———— • ◆ • ————

An England rugby union international who made his debut on 6 June 1998 v Australia, when England lost 76–0 to the hosts, a record defeat. For many years this hard-tackling open-side flanker has played his club rugby in France, and has recently and quite unusually, returned to amateur status from being a professional, but continues to hold his place at the cutting edge of the French game.

It was a particularly violent rugby match even by the desperate local standards, played in the scorching afternoon heat as far south as France would allow.

At the end of the match, despite having spent 80 minutes trying to slug chunks out of each other, an Englishman and a Frenchman were overcoming their cultural differences in the tried-and-tested manner, courtesy of several litres of vin de table.

However, before long the generations-old rivalry between their respective nations comes back to the surface and the Frenchman couldn't resist boasting to his new English friend, 'Deed you know, een ma coontry, we 'ave 92 ways of making love?'

The Englishman looks nervously around at the pretty local girls who had started to hover around the bar and started to feel a little intimidated for the first time that day.

Reduced to a whisper, he admits nervously to this French Latin lover, '92 ways of making love. That's incredible! In England, we only have one.'

The Frenchman smiles: 'Ah, yes? And wat wood zat be?'

The Englishman, slightly embarrassed: 'Well, there's a man and a woman, and ...'

'MON DIEU!' shouts the Frenchman. 'Number 93!'

BUDGE POUNTNEY

A Scotland rugby union international flanker, he has captained his country and has won 28 caps to date. He plays his club rugby for Northampton Saints.

Jim Telfer is part of Scottish rugby folklore, hugely inspirational, a superb coach but also hard, demanding, austere, and something of a disciplinarian. If he said, 'Jump,' you replied, 'How high?' What he said went – no discussions – and certainly no arguments.

Just before the last World Cup, Scotland went up to Troon on a training camp to get away from it all and to focus our minds on the huge task of playing in the ultimate rugby competition in the world. We had been training hard and, as a consequence, we all used to have a lie-in whenever possible. Now, Telfer got irritated by this so he decided that there was to be no more slovenly behaviour – no more lie-ins. He ordered us up at 7.00 a.m. sharp the next day to go for a walk, to contemplate the battles ahead.

So, bang on the button we were marched out by Telfer to start this walk. We had been issued with great long coats that looked like trench coats, and with caps over our heads to ward off the cold. We looked like some army on the march. When Big Jim barked that we should get into pairs, the scene was set. We had decided not to talk for the whole walk but unfortunately this was going to prove very difficult as I had been paired with Stuart Grimes – someone who has a complete inability to keep a straight face and not laugh.

Off we walked, Telfer in the lead. All remained hush for a while as we continued to keep pace with Telfer, who led the way, a ball under the crook of one arm – quite a picture.

After a while though, a faint whistling started, led by the front runners of Doddie Weir and Gary Armstrong, which got progressively louder – a well-known tune at that. Sniggering then began to emanate from the long line of marching pairs of Scottish internationals. Telfer continued to lead the procession. Then the words starting drifting towards him that accompanied this famous whistled tune …

'Hitler, has only got one ball, the other … '

PS It has been rumoured that Jim found this hugely amusing. This hasn't ever been proved though …

DAVID POWELL

———————— • ◆ • ————————

A former England rugby union international prop who
won 11 caps between 1966 and 1971. Powell was also
a Lions tourist and is now the head groundsman
for Northampton Saints.

When I told my father, who was a farmer like me, that I had won my first England cap, he immediately replied:

'Where's the match?'

Thinking that he may be keen to come to the game, I replied:

'It's at home, at Twickenham against Wales.'

'That's good,' he said, 'you will only want Saturday afternoon off work. Oh, and as it is at home you'll be able to milk the cows that morning, and of course Sunday morning too!'

Which of course, I did ….

JULIE PULLIN

Britain's former no. 1 women's tennis player, Julie competed for Great Britain in the 2000 Olympic Games in Sydney.

It was the opening ceremony of the Sydney 2000 Olympics and I was lucky enough to have qualified to represent Great Britain in the doubles. Although not officially allowed, everyone had cameras and mobile phones with them. It was the most amazing feeling entering the stadium with Team GB led by Matthew Pinsent and, having walked half-way round the track waving to the crowds, my phone rang. It was my brother to let me know he had just seen me on TV and asked what I was doing at the moment! He had not realised the ceremony was live but on being told where I was, he delightedly replied, 'Do you mean to say I'm actually walking round the stadium with you?'

Q

NIALL QUINN

A Republic of Ireland footballer, he is Ireland's all-time lead-ing goal scorer. He has also played for Arsenal, Manchester City and Sunderland. He famously gave the proceeds of his testimonial match, totalling £1,000,000, to charity.

At Arsenal Paul Mariner was getting a rollicking from one of the coaches. The coach told him, 'What you know about coaching you could write on the back of a postage stamp.'

One of the other players shouted, 'Yeh, with a paintbrush!'

SCOTT QUINNELL

A Welsh rugby union international no. 8, he has won 50 caps to date and has captained his country. He was a Lions tourist in 1997 and 2001. He also had a spell in rugby league playing for Wigan.

On the 2001 Lions tour to Australia, we trained hard, and the games were tough, but we also had a little time out of the rugby environment in which to experience various tourist attractions that the country offered. One day out, me, Rob Howley, Daffyd James and Brian O'Driscoll were at a zoo and were being shown a snake. This was not your average little wriggler, this was big.

'This is a 25 ft Asian Python,' said the snake handler. 'This type of snake is capable of eating goats, lambs and is reputed to have eaten humans as well.'

We all took a step backwards, as this great thing was not too far away. We pretended to take a great interest in the snake, though keen to get as far away as possible whilst not seeming rude. A photographer who was working with the Lions then came up:

'Right lads, let's have a picture, all four of you holding the snake! No getting out of it, you're all doing it.'

Knowing we had to have our photo taken, I immediately rushed forward and grabbed hold of the snake's tail. Rob and Brian soon caught on and stepped smartly forward. Daffyd James couldn't quite work out why we were so keen to embrace this huge great python, having been so wary of it seconds before.

Only then did his face drop. Brian and Rob had grabbed the middle section of the snake, and there was only one place left for Daffyd in the photo. The action end! He had to hold the snake by its head, flicking tongue and gleaming eyes.

The photo is fantastic, three grinning Lions, and one not!

*   *   *

I am a born and bred Welshman, having been brought up on a diet of rugby. My dad played for Wales and I am hugely passionate about the game. I love it.

When I was 18 I lived for the sport (and still do). I was on the bench for Llanelli and was keen to make a good impression. I had yet to make my debut and was busting at the seams to get on the pitch and show everyone what I could do, to play for the much-vaunted Llanelli and prove myself.

Half the game was gone and still no nod from the coach to take off my tracksuit. (One of those all-in-one suits, that unzip down the middle – like a baby suit.) I continued to stretch, to look keen and hungry. The match continued. I was desperate to get on. I had dreamed about charging on to the field and playing for the club.

There was suddenly an injury, the player did not look as though he could carry on, this was my big chance. A massive crowd, all watching. I looked at the coach, and eventually he gave me the OK to go on.

This was the moment, the dream.

I unzipped my tracksuit, stepped out, all ready to charge into battle. Something though felt wrong, something wasn't right. I looked down.

I had revealed myself to the world. Shirt – yes, socks and boots – yes, gumshield yes, I had forgotten only one thing … my shorts.

Not a thunderous entrance to top-flight rugby, but an embarrassed exit, to find the missing article of clothing!

R

NEAL RADFORD

An England and Worcestershire cricketer who made his debut for England v India in 1986. Radford was a right-arm fast medium bowler and took 994 first class wickets.

While playing in South Africa, we, the Transvaal team, were doing a session of signing bats and memorabilia, when someone noticed a problem. A young Afrikaans lad – Stephen Van der Merwe, was doing this for the first time and was signing his name on the bat handle, not on the blade of the bat. When questioned about this, the embarrassed lad responded by saying with a broad Afrikaans accent, 'But how did you know it was me?'

The English Amateur champion in 1964, Ray captured his first World Professional title in 1970 and went on to dominate the decade by winning the World title on another five occasions, including a remarkable quartet of successes from 1973 to 1976. A former President of the World Professional Billiards and Snooker Association, Ray remains a snooker legend and managed to reach the semi finals of the World Championship in 1985, at the age of 53.

A man walked into a supermarket with a basket and proceeded to place in it one sausage, one rasher of bacon, one egg, one onion, one tomato and then went to the checkout. The checkout lady flashed the items through the till and said, 'You're not married, are you?'

The man replied, 'You are right, I am single, how did you know that?'

'Because you are the ugliest man I've ever seen!'

* * *

I was playing the 5th hole at Churtston Golf Course, which runs parallel with the 14th (both par 5). When I was about to play my fairway shot, a man walked across from the 14th, peers at me and says, 'You're that snooker chap.'

I said:

'That's right, but I'm playing golf.'

'One question that always bothered me,' he said. 'Can you tell me the main difference between golf and snooker?'

I looked up under my eyebrows and said, 'I've never lost a snooker ball.'

DAVID REES

An England rugby union international winger who made his full England debut in the 15–15 draw against Australia at Twickenham in 1997. Rees has 11 caps to date and plays his club rugby at Bristol.

I have been lucky enough to play against some fantastic players but arguably the most famous is Jonah Lomu. I was opposite him in an enthralling 26–26 draw against the All Blacks at Twickenham in 1997 and even managed to sneak a try past him. The preparations, though, tell a different story ....

Clive Woodward was leading a team meeting with the backs and Jonah's name came up.

'Right Reesy, how are we going to deal with this guy Jonah Lomu?'

'OK, Clive, I'm gonna angle my run so I push him towards the touch line and use it as an extra man, just forcing him out for a line-out.'

'OK. What happens if he cuts inside you?'

'Well, I'll angle it so that he's running back towards our cover defence and Kyran Bracken will be there to help me smother him and bring him down.'

'Uh-huh. And what if he comes straight at you?'

'Well, if he runs straight at me I'll get some crap on the ground and throw it in his face, blinding him.'

'What? But there won't be any crap on the ground.'

'When he's running straight at me, Clive, yes there will!'

DEAN RICHARDS

*A former England rugby union international, he is the most
capped no. 8 in the history of the game with 48 caps.
A Lions tourist in 1989 and 1993 and a World Cup finalist
in 1991. He is now the Director of Rugby with Leicester
Tigers, for whom he has masterminded four back-to-back
League titles and unprecedented back-to-back European
Cup wins.*

We were on tour back in 1991 and had just left Australia. Our
last port of call on our way home was Fiji – one last international
prior to home. The night before the match a few of us
were relaxing at our hotel – The Regent – and we ended up
having a beer. A beautiful setting, a live band playing in the
background … perfect. Well, one beer led to other … and so
on. By the end of the evening we were right on form, the rest of
the area had cleared and the band had gone home, but we
hadn't finished.

Someone spotted that the drums, guitar and other instruments
had unwisely been left unattended and it seemed too
good an opportunity to miss – an impromptu jamming session.
Up we got, onto the stage. Dewi Morris on the guitar,
John Hall with the maracas, Ollie Redmond on the tambourine,
myself on drums and John Olver on the mike, ready
to let rip.

No sound, though – no good. Olver then looked to the side
of the stage and spotted what he was after – all the switches to
the amps. Over he strode to turn them all on. Unbeknown to
him, the coach, Geoff Cooke, started wandering through the
bushes towards us.

Olver stepped up to the mike, ready for the concert. He raised
his head and put his mouth to the mike: 'HELLO WEMBLEY!'

Watching, unimpressed, was Cooke. On stage was Olver.

Our lead singer turned round, confident in the fact that his fellow musicians would be with him, only to find he was alone. We had seen Cooke making his way towards us, and had slipped away. An awkward silence for John Olver, the only background accompaniment he got that night was our laughter in the distance!

* * *

It was just two days before the 1991 World Cup final and myself, John Olver, Mike Teague, Jeff Probyn and Dewi Morris were kindly invited for a bit of duck flighting. 'Perfect,' we thought, nothing too strenuous, just a breath of fresh air, and a chance to take our minds off what was the biggest game of our careers. The man in charge – Graham Mackay. He stitched us up good and proper ....

'Well lads, we'll just a walk a corner or two, through a few gullies ....'

We ended up walking about ten miles, this of course just 48 hours before taking on the Ozzies, tramping along, we were absolutely boxed, and eventually were just coming down this last little bit where we saw a gentle valley. The dog was racing around ahead and managed to put this bird up just in front of us. John Olver, grateful for some sport, latched onto the duck:

BANG!

Did he down the duck? No chance. The only thing that dropped was Mike Teague – like a sack of sh**, straight to the ground. If you ever see the photograph of Teaguey during the game, there is the mark, just above his eye – testament not to the great battle on the pitch – but Olver and our duck flighting off it!

DAVID RIPLEY

A Northamptonshire wicketkeeper who can boast over 250 first-class dismissals.

West Indian fast bowler Wayne Daniel hit David Steele in the chest area. David was a very tough competitor and tried to show no pain to Wayne, who smiled and said, 'Rub it man, I know it hurts.'

*   *   *

Sledging was made famous by the Australians. Dennis Lillee had a year with Northamptonshire. It was a great honour to play with him. A couple of his clinics from the year (obviously, with a few choice expletives deleted):

'Where did you get that technique? The back of a cereal packet?'

'I've seen better batters on fish, mate!'

IAN ROBERTSON

A former Scotland rugby union international, who also represented Watsonians and Cambridge University, Ian is now a BBC radio rugby commentator.

On the 1983 Lions Tour to New Zealand, at breakfast in Wanganui during the first week, Donal Lenihan rushes into the dining room and says, 'Quick, quick. I'm late for training. Can you please get me some toast and rashers of bacon?' The waitress apologises and says, 'You won't believe it – we are out of bacon.'

Donal looks aghast and stares at her in disbelief: 'Three million sheep in New Zealand – how can you be out of bacon?'

*   *   *

Second row forwards are not always intellectual giants. A certain second row who happened to be captain of England was asked at a press conference on the eve of a match against New Zealand:

'Some people think the All Blacks are invincible – does that worry you?' He replied, 'Of course it worries me if the All Blacks are invincible. I mean, it stands to reason, if we can't see them, how can we beat them?'

JOHN ROBERTSON

A former Scotland international footballer, Robertson was a double European Cup-winner with Nottingham Forest, first in 1979 when Forest beat Malmö, then in 1980 when he scored in the final against Hamburg.

A man walks into a bar and orders a pint of beer.

'£1.80,' says the barman.

'I've no money,' says the man, 'but I have a talking dog here and if I got the dog to talk, can I have the beer?'

The barman replies:

'If you get that dog to talk, you can have free drink all afternoon.' The man sits the dog on the end of the bar:

'Okay Fido, if a man has ten pints of vodka and ten pints of whisky, how does he feel the following day?'

'Ruff,' says the dog.

'No way!' exclaimed the barman. 'Any dog can do that.'

'OK,' says the man, 'give me another go – Fido is brilliant at sport. Fido, if a man playing golf hits a shot down the fairway and it takes a bad bounce and runs into the long grass, where does it finish?'

'Ruff,' came the reply.

'Right, that's it,' said the barman, 'don't try to take the Mickey out of me.'

'OK,' said the man, 'give me one last go. Fido, who played in goal for Scotland in the 1986 World Cup in Mexico?'

'Ruff,' replied the dog.

'Right,' said the barman, 'that's enough,' and he kicked the man and dog onto the street. He was just about to close the pub door when he heard the dog say to the man:

'I made a mistake there, it was Jim Leighton, wasn't it?'

WOMEN'S
INTERNATIONAL
SOCCER

"I KNOW THE MATCH IS ALMOST OVER. I'VE ONLY COME TO WATCH THEM SWAP SHIRTS."

MARK ROBSON

With over 20 years' experience as a sports presenter and commentator, he has worked for Sky TV, Eurosport, the BBC and ITV, specialising in motor cycling, tennis, rugby and golf.

The other two lads were very famous and that was the problem. You see, Mark Robson wasn't and, in fact, he still isn't! It was the Rugby World Cup of 1995 and, much to my surprise, I was engaged to work as the third-choice commentator for the ITV network. A big gig for me, even if all the matches were 'off tube' – in other words done from a tiny booth complete with miniature TV. There would be no actual commentary from the stadiums but still it was quite a career break and if anything happened to the senior commentators I would step in. Anyway, we all flew out to Jo'burg with your little Irishman feeling rather Johnny Big Potatoes. After all, this was the ultimate stage.

Commentators 1 and 2 were the redoubtable John Taylor and the experienced Chris Rea, both former British Lions. On arrival we were all ferried to the massive offices of the host broadcaster SABC for a welcome party and there I was, surrounded by all the big cheeses in South African television.

Of course it's a true rugby nation and all these guys knew John Taylor and Chris Rea by reputation and couldn't wait to shake their hands.

The flat Afrikaans vowels came thick and fast:

'It's windarfil to hev yoo here in oor kintry,' they blundered, their biltong-boosted bellies heaving with excitement. How important I felt! A big exec was soon striding towards me: 'Who are yoo?' he barked

'Stand-by commentator,' I replied.

'Nice to meet you, Stan,' he said. Johnny Big Potatoes had been mashed!

* * *

A long time ago, back in the days of black-and-white television, RTE, the Irish national channel based in Dublin, decided they should get up to speed on the technology front. Not right up to speed, but certainly on the heels of their big-wig British rivals.

Various television stations had been toying with slow-motion action replays and one or two had used them during matches. RTE thought that the time had come for them to also do replays. The production team, in liaison with management, chose a Republic of Ireland international soccer match to announce their arrival on the high-tech scene, which was fine, except that their detailed planning hadn't included informing ... the commentator. Which was not so good, especially for him.

The commentator shall remain nameless, but to set the scene, this chap was preparing for his *first* international commentary and was already feeling, shall we say, rather vulnerable. Now, RTE didn't want to launch themselves right into the deep stuff so they thought that, instead of slow-motion replays, they would do them at normal speed. 'Less chance of a cock-up, we'll ease ourselves in gently,' they thought. So the match begins and the commentator is commentating. The Republic of Ireland break away down the left-hand side:

'Away go Ireland,' he roared. 'It's Liam Brady with the ball. A marvellous shimmy from the little genius.' So far, so good.

'Brady looks up ... Don Givens is in space at the far post. Chippy [Brady] chips it in.' Excellent choice of words.

'Up goes Givens ... a bullet header ... IT'S THERE!!!!! 1–0 to the Republic of Ireland.'

Now, commentators are slaves to the monitor beside them, so they can refer to close-ups or crowd shots the director might give them and, like any good broadcaster, our man was now glued to the little screen at his elbow. The adrenalin, remember, was surging through every cell of his twitching frame and now he was on a roll ... brash, confident and ready for anything.

Next came a close-up of Brady:

'And there's the man who made the goal possible.'

A close-up of Givens: 'It was Deadly Don who flashed that ferocious header into the roof of the net.' Fabulous stuff.

Then the director plays in the action replay and our commentator sees Brady cross the ball for Givens to score.

Our commentator then says, 'I don't believe it ... he's done it again!!!!!'

TIM RODBER

A former England rugby union international, winning 44 caps between 1992 and 1999, and was Lions tourist in 1997.

The Lions had just lost to the Blue Bulls in Pretoria in 1997 and Ian McGeechan asked me to captain the midweek team to play the Cats in Jo'burg.

I was told by Geech it was going to be hell. There we were on Monday morning before the Wednesday game at altitude, getting beasted around the park by Jim 'Creamy' Telfer. Jim was never a man to pull his punches and if you watched the 'Living with the Lions' video you would have remembered the scrummage session when my language was particularly 'colourful.'

Anyway, the forwards had been going for about an hour and a half. By now, we were completely knackered, Jim had turned a bright red colour from the screaming and shouting he had been doing. The forwards had had enough. Jim decided we were going to do a rucking drill, so all the forwards gathered behind the ball carrier to face the pads for rucking drills.

By now the bag holders were getting very worked up, as they were the team that had lost a few days before and you knew they were going to try to take their frustrations out on me and the tired bunch of forwards I was with.

The ball carrier was the then golden bollocks of Scottish rugby and Jim's right hand man, Rob Wainwright. Jim shouted at him and off we began as Rob crashed into the first pad. He dropped the ball ... Jim went ballistic.

'You f***ing idiot, get back to the start.'

So back we trooped, exhausted and fed up. 'GO, ROB, GO!' we shouted, so off he charged and down went the ball again.

Telfer went cataclysmic.

Of course, by now the shouting and screaming had not gone unnoticed by the journalists and backs who were having a nice

231

cup of tea and a chat. They finished their drinks and gathered to what would surely be the explosion that could result in the heart failure of 'Creamy'. Sure enough, Rob started again and everyone held their breath. Down went the ball.

'Wainwright, bloody Wainwright!!! You're like a lighthouse in the desert ... brilliant but fucking useless!!!'

The whole squad fell about laughing and Jim, to his credit, stopped training.

In that one moment the squad came closer, Jim gained massive respect from the players and the stall was set for the rest of the tour ... we didn't lose again midweek.

PETER RODRIGUES

*A former Welsh international footballer and Southampton
captain who lifted the FA Cup with the Saints in 1976.*

The first story relates to a game in the Cup-Winners' Cup for Southampton against Carrick Rangers (Ireland). One of the Carrick players got injured after ten minutes, the two stretcher bearers came on and proceeded to place the player on the stretcher. They then got hold of the handles and lifted the player up,

"Oh dear," they said. They were facing each other.

Obviously one had to turn around, and as he did, he tried balancing the player on his knee he tried to turn. The player fell off the stretcher in even more agony. As all good Irish people do, they found it quite amusing.

* * *

The other story involved myself, playing for Sheffield Wednesday against Bournemouth. I can remember making a tackle just in front of the dug-out, I collapsed in a heap and immediately thought I had broken my leg, it just went numb from the knee down. They put me on the stretcher and carried me to the dressing room. They couldn't get the stretcher around one of the corners so I decided to get off. Reluctantly and in a lot of pain, I was helped off by the physio, and in the process I jerked my knee quite sharply. Well, you wouldn't believe it but the numbness went and I walked back into the dressing room, and could have continued the match. I had trapped a nerve in my knee, which caused the numbness.

DAVE ROGERS

*A sports photographer for 28 years, during which time he
has covered six Lions tours.*

The Hong Kong 7s is one of the most famous tournaments in the world, almost as much for its off-pitch partying as its on-pitch playing, but there is one tournament that will always stand out more than any other, the year Jonah Lomu first played and announced himself into the rugby world – never to be forgotten. He was quite sensational, never before had such raw power and brute strength blitzed opposition as he did that week.

He was, of course, the star of the whole tournament. After the final, which New Zealand won, the players went on a victory lap; we were busy taking pictures for all the newspapers across the world. It was, though, proving quite a challenge to get a clear shot of the men in black, especially Jonah, because the pitch had been well and truly invaded by fans who had been on the piss all day.

Eventually three photographers, myself included, managed to elbow our way through the heaving mass of pissed-up Kiwis to get Eric Rush and Jonah Lomu together. We asked them to pose with the trophy. On one hand Eric Rush, an established legend of New Zealand rugby, on the other side, the star of the future, Jonah – a great photograph.

We had one problem, this young New Zealand fan, who was totally arseholed, kept poking his head up behind the two players and ruining our photo.

One of three photographers, Colin Elsey, politely asked the fan if he could move aside so we could get the picture.

No luck, this fella still kept poking his head around, making faces.

The second photographer, Peter Bush, a veteran Kiwi photographer then said:

'Look mate, could you just get out of the way – just for a moment, then you can celebrate all night.'

No chance, the young fan kept mucking about behind the two players, shoving his way between Rush and Lomu, ducking back and making gestures. After about two minutes of being shoved and pushed by the drunken crowd, still no usable photograph, this lad was still mucking about behind the two stars.

I was fed up:

'Just f**k off will you, how old are you anyway?'

'Nineteen,' Jonah replied.

*　*　*

On the 1989 Lions tour to Australia, the players had a day out and were invited to the Royal Perth Yacht Club. It was just after Australia had lost in the final to the US in the Americas Cup yacht races.

Not all the tour party went along but among the group were a few Welsh backs. The President of the yacht club was showing them around the club and took them onto the *Kookaburra 2*, this beautiful, streamlined racing machine, the hope of the nation that had just failed to beat the Yanks. Australia had spent about 25,000,000 dollars on this project to try to win the cup back, but although proud to have been a part of such a famous head-to-head race, were at the same time gutted to have lost to *Stars and Stripes*.

The captain of *Kookaburra 2* was then introduced to the players.

'Do a bit of racing then, do you?' Asked one of the Welshmen innocently.

'Yeh, mate. Actually we've just been in the Americas Cup where we sailed against the Americans.'

'How did you get on, then?' Asked the second Welsh back, pleased that they were bonding with this Australian.

'Umm, we came second,' came the reply.

Third Welshman:

'Second. That's bloody good, isn't it!'

TONY RUDLIN

An international motor racing driver, and team manager for Lotus and the Argentinian national team. He has had nine novels published and is now a successful film scriptwriter/producer.

In 1968 Jack Coliver was entered in a race at Rheims. Race preparation was done in a square about half a mile from the circuit. I was Team Manager for the Lotus entry. When the time came to go to the track, I opted to drive the car myself. Unfortunately I promptly got lost! I circled around, asking incredulous locals the way to the circuit for about 20 minutes. When I finally arrived at the track, both the clutch and the engine were well cooked. Jack was not amused.

S

JAMIE SALMON

———— •◆• ————

*A former rugby union international and the only player ever
to have represented both New Zealand and England.*

Bob Hiller, the England and Harlequins full back, was playing
for his club and during one game was continually talking to the
referee regarding the validity of his decisions.

After a Quins try, Bob was preparing for the conversion and
said something else to the ref.

The ref is fed up by now: 'Look here, Hiller, who's refereeing
this match, me or you?'

Hiller's reply: 'That's the problem, neither of us.'

* * *

Having already played for New Zealand, my first cap when I
got selected for England was, ironically, against the All Blacks.
It also happened to be against most of the guys that I had
played with when I had the silver fern on my chest.

Murray Mexted, the no. 8, rang up the day before the first
Test to say, 'Well done' etc. Also, he said, the guys were looking
forward to having a few beers with me after the Test match. It

was a very pleasant chat from a former team-mate, but just as we were saying goodbye, Mexted said:

'Oh, one more thing Jamie, if you come back on the switch during the game, I will take your f***ing head off!'

DEAN SAMPSON

Castleford and Great Britain rugby league international.

This guy walks into a sports shop in Castleford. The shop assistant, a teenage girl, comes out to serve him.

'A packet of condoms, please,' asks the man.

'I'm sorry Sir,' She replies.

'A packet of condoms, please,' he says. 'You know, a packet of three, something for the weekend.'

'Sorry Sir,' replies the girl. 'This is a sports shop, we don't sell them.'

'Can you get the manager then, please?' asks the customer. Off goes the girl and a minute or so later a middle-aged man appears who is the manager.

'Ah, thank God,' says the customer. 'This really is very, very embarrassing, I actually wanted to buy a Wakefield Trinity Wildcats shirt ….'

HANS SEGERS

*A former Nottingham Forest and Wimbledon FC goalkeeper
and the current Tottenham Hotspur goalkeeping coach.*

Early in one football season we travelled up to West Ham
United. My manager that time was Mr Brian Clough and it was
my early days at Nottingham Forest where Cloughie was a
well-respected man. Well, one Saturday we hit traffic on the
M25 – three lanes into two lanes, with the inside lane coned
off. The traffic was at a standstill. The driver, Albert, said to
Clough, 'Manager, we're not going to be there on time.'

Clough: 'Stop the coach.' He stepped out, took ten cones off
the inside lane and jumped back in.

'Drive into the inside lane,' he told Albert. Albert did. After all,
Cloughie was the boss. We drove into the inside lane, Cloughie
jumped out and put the cones back. We drove four miles in the
coned-off lane, past all the traffic until we saw the police, blue
lights on top, coming towards us. They stopped the coach,
Cloughie went out and started chatting with them. The end result?
We finished with a police escort to West Ham United. It was then I
really knew that Cloughie was popular all over England.

FERGUS SLATTERY

*A former Ireland rugby union international who is the third
most capped Irishman of all time with 61 caps. He has
captained his country and was a Lions tourist in 1974.*

During the 1977 Lions tour to New Zealand, Peter Wheeler wrote
home to his wife on day 32, 'It has only rained twice since we
arrived. The first time for 21 days, and the second time for 11 days.'

* * *

Moss Keane playing for Ireland against England: 'First half spent pushing in the line-outs and the second half jumping in the scrums.'

ALAN SMITH

———— •◆• ————

A former England international footballer, winning 13 caps. He played for Leicester and Arsenal, winning two League titles, the FA Cup, the Cup-Winners' Cup and two 'Golden Boot's.

Arsenal were playing at Highbury when our striker, Perry Groves, got injured. After he limped to the sideline for treatment, a stretcher was brought round to carry him back to the dressing room.

As the game carried on, we noticed a bit of commotion on the track. Grovesy, somehow, had fallen off the stretcher and with an agonised look on his face was trying to clamber back on. The crowd thought it was hilarious and so did his teammates. Injured? He never heard the last of it.

* * *

I was stopping at Burnham Beeches with England. One morning I came out for training, jumped on the bus as normal and settled down for the short trip to Bisham Abbey.

As the coach made its way down a country lane, I noticed my car abandoned on the verge. Overnight, someone had obviously stolen it. All the players thought this was highly comical. Not only had the thief abandoned the car, he hadn't even touched any of my music tapes.

'Sums up your taste, Alan!' The lads chuckled.

JAMES M SMITH

Football manager.

A player is speaking to his manager about tactics: 'I am confused, I do not know whether I am coming or going.'

'Son,' said the manager, 'I can help you there, you are going.'

* * *

A penguin goes into a bar and says, 'Barman, have you seen my father?'

'What does he look like?' says the barman.

ROBIN SMITH

An England international cricketer between 1988 and 1996, with a Test average of 45. He hit nine Test hundreds and has captained Hampshire. He is known as the 'Judge'.

In the cricketing world there's nothing quite like beating the Australians. Unfortunately, during my career, I've always come up against a pretty awesome Australian side and haven't enjoyed too many occasions when an England side came out on top. Having said that, I've always enjoyed playing against the old enemy! I've always respected their attitude to the game, which is to be disciplined and to play hard on the field.

Over the years I've enjoyed my battles with the Aussies and in particular that great big ugly bastard, Merv Hughes! An incident I remember vividly was a game played at Lord's during the 1983 Ashes series. Allan Border won the toss and chose to bat. Once again, Australia helped themselves to a feast of runs and decided to put us out of our misery and declare just after lunch on the second day, having scored 550.

We capitulated again in the first innings and were made to follow on – this didn't come as a great surprise to our critics. In the second innings, David Gower and I walked out to bat on Sunday, the fourth morning of the Test. Merv Hughes opened up at the Pavilion End, and bowled with great pace and accuracy for the first hour of the day. Unfortunately I was the unlucky one, having to face him at the Nursery End. I played and missed regularly and you can imagine the verbal abuse I was receiving from the slip cordon and an angry Merv Hughes! After I played and missed a further three consecutive balls, he came down the wicket, looked at me, and said, 'Oi, Smithy! I thought they said you could bat – you are ******* useless.'

There wasn't much I could say at the time because he was absolutely right. That morning I was struggling. Two balls later, he ran in and I think through sheer frustration, he tried to bowl one too short and too fast. The ball was badly directed and in the perfect area for a square cut. I managed to hit this one in the middle of the bat, and the ball raced over the outfield, up the hill, smashed into the advertising boards and rolled back down to mid-off, who lobbed the ball back to the *furious* bowler.

I don't know exactly why I ran down the wicket for a single, because as soon as I hit the ball, I knew it was going to be four all the way. When I arrived at the bowler's end, I said, 'Oi, Merv!'

As he span around with anger, saliva, sweat and snot dripping from that great big droopy moustache, I thought to myself, 'Oops, what have you just done?' The game came to standstill, so I had to think of something to say quickly. My reply shot out without really thinking: 'We make a great pair, don't we Merv? I can't bat and you certainly can't f***ing bowl!'

As you can imagine, during our playing days, we never really saw eye to eye. But since his retirement, we've become good friends and always enjoy reminiscing about our many battles out on the field.

WAYNE SMITH

A New Zealand rugby union coach in 2000 and 2001, he is now Director of Rugby at Northampton Saints .

I was coaching in Italy in 1986 at a club called Casale Sul Sile, and had only been there a short time. I was working closely with the team manager called Dino Menegazzi. He was a cracking fella but was a little gullible. There is about a 12-hour time difference between Italy and New Zealand and we were going to Rome to play the local team. The two of us were in a coffee shop talking on the day of the game and the chat strayed to home. He said, 'What time would it be in New Zealand now?' He was trying really hard to grasp the time difference.

I looked at my watch and said, 'Well, it would be about 1 o'clock tomorrow morning.'

'Nah, it can't be tomorrow down there, really?' He replied.

'Well if I rang my Mum and Dad,' I replied, 'they could tell us if we won the game or not.'

He scratched his head and looked at me and suddenly slammed his fist on the table and said, 'Ring them and if we haven't won, we won't play.'

STEVE SMITH-ECCLES

A jump jockey who was the winner of three consecutive Champion Hurdles in the 1980s on the horse See You Then.

My track record in the Grand National is not great. I have fallen at Bechers Brook seven times. The last time I was way out at the back of the field with John Francome and was in the process of telling him a joke. I was just about to deliver the punch line when up popped Bechers and down I went.

Through a gashed forehead and red haze, I saw this horse and jockey trotting back towards me. Lo and behold – John Francome. My first thoughts were – what a mate! He's come back to see if I'm all right. His opening line was, 'What the f*** did the monkey say to the gorilla?'

He only came back for the punch line. Some mate!

* * *

Jockeys take pee pills for rapid weight loss. I was lucky with my weight but did have to take them on one occasion. But I got my timing wrong; they did not take effect till I was down at the start on my horse. I had to go! So, I asked the starter's assistant to hold my horse whilst I had a pee!

This pee was captured on TV and it took so long – it just trickled out! I was reported to the stewards and fined £50 for delaying the start!

DAVID SNELL

*A former professional golfer who has achieved a hole-in-one
20 times and won the 1959 News of the World PGA
MatchPlay Championship. He has become a noted designer
and builder of golf courses and plays on the European
Seniors Tour.*

While playing in the Open at Lytham St Annes, Hedley
Muscroft and myself were training on the Golden Mile in
Blackpool. Early in the week we noticed a booth featuring 'Big
Chief Wise Owl', who guaranteed to answer any sporting question or pay a forfeit. We joined the queue with the idea of
posing an obscure golf question and thus win the prize. When
we reached our turn, Hedley asked:

'Who won the Open in 1896?'

Quick as a flash the Chief replied:

'Harry Vardon.'

We were obviously very impressed and left to continue our
training. Two years later we were back in Lytham for the Pringle
Tournament. Visiting Blackpool again one evening, who should
be walking towards us but Big Chief Wise Owl in his full
regalia. As he came up to us I greeted him in his native tongue:

'How!' I said. He replied:

'After a 36 hole play-off with JH Taylor.'

*   *   *

Playing in a recent Seniors Tour Pro-Am, one of my partners
topped his drive just a few yards off his tee. He duffed his
second, shanked his third, topped his fourth, then thinned an
iron to just short of the first green. He then picked up his ball.

'Why did you not finish the hole?' I asked, as we were not
holding anyone up.

His reply: 'It's just that my short game is terrible.'

GARETH SOUTHGATE

An England international footballer, he has won 45 caps to date. He has also played for Crystal Palace, Aston Villa and Middlesbrough.

I went to watch a match with my wife and the family of a friend (who was playing). People started turning around to ask for autographs, which is always flattering but can start to interfere with your enjoyment of an event. By now the game had kicked off and yet still I was being passed scraps of paper and programmes to sign.

I obliged, but must confess I was getting irritable as I tried to watch the game. A flag was passed along and then a ticket.

'Pen?' I asked down the line, somewhat abruptly, and a pen was duly passed along the line.

'What's his name?' I asked my friend's wife, and the query was passed down the line.

'To John, all the best, Gareth Southgate', I wrote and passed the ticket back along the line.

Out of the corner of my eye I see the guy look at the ticket and start to edge along the row. I'm just about to say to him:

'Look mate, no disrespect, but I'm trying to watch the game', when he says apologetically:

'Excuse me, I'm very sorry but you're in my seat!'

DAVID SPEEDIE

A former Scotland international footballer, winning 10 caps, he made his international debut in a 1–0 win over England in 1985. He also played for Darlington, Chelsea, Liverpool, Coventry, and Blackburn Rovers.

Just advertised: Bungee jumping from hot air balloon, £5 per head. Taliban go free! No strings attached.

* * *

Three Irishmen apply for a job for which no Irish were allowed. First, Paddy goes for interview.

The interviewer looks at him and said:

'Name?'

Paddy replies:

'Marks & Spencer.'

'Get out, you're Irish,' shouted the interviewer. Murphy goes in, interviewer again: 'Name?'

'Freeman Hardy Willis,' he replied.

'Get out, you're Irish.' Then the third Irishman then goes in. Interviewer:

'Name?'

'Ken,' he replies. The interview continues for 15 minutes. Finally the interviewer said:

'Great, you've got the job, you start on Monday. What's your full name?'

'Ken Tucky Fried Chicken,' he replied.

MIKE STEPHENSON

A former Great Britain rugby league international hooker, winning the World Cup in 1972. He captained the Dewsbury side that won the League in 1973 and played for the Penrith Panthers in Australia. He is now a Sky TV commentator and analyst.

When I went to Australia in 1973, it was a world record transfer fee, sounds ludicrous now, but it was for £20,000. In rugby league at that time it was a phenomenal amount of money and the new side, Penrith Panthers, were wanting their money's worth. In the five years that I was there I found it was the toughest rugby I have ever encountered. It was nicknamed 'Thugby League', not rugby league. I found out why in my first game.

There were some real tough nuts and one man who played for South Sydney, George Piggins, happened to be my opposite number that day. George was one of the nicest blokes you could ever wish to meet off the pitch, but on the pitch, well, something obviously went off in his head. He was a real competitor. The match started, with a lot of hype about my debut. Every time there was a scrum, there was going to be a clash of heads between George and me. Every time there was a knock on, I thought oh no, here we go again. There was another scrum, and it was quite loose and I found myself on the floor. It just happened that one leg went left, the other leg went right, I was flat on my back. George just happened to be above me and as he fell, he just happened to put his knee into my groin. I couldn't see, I could hardly breath ….

The doc raced out and I was pointing to my groin, and still couldn't speak.

'It appears that he has fractured his rib and maybe punctured his lung. Get him on the stretcher and let's get him off.' When we got into the changing room, they had already taken off my shirt, looking for the rib injury, when I managed to speak:

'It's my balls, it's my balls.' So they cut off my shorts and looked down.

'Christ, grab hold of him.' The physio and rubber came over.

'What's wrong? What's wrong?' There I was naked except for my socks and boots.

'I want to stiffen your body as hard as you can,' said the doc.

'What? Why?'

'Just do as you are told.'

They grabbed either side of me, stood me up and shook me

up and down until on the fourth judder, my right testicle popped back down. The pain was excruciating – from the frying pan into the fire.

The half-time whistle had just sounded, the team came in and the coach wandered over.

'Look, I need you, you must continue playing, how are you feeling?'

'I've had a pretty bad knock, I think I might struggle.'

The coach looked at the doc and he said:

'He's just had a testicle impaled inside his body: if he does it again, he could rupture it.'

'Well, there's no way in the world that I'm risking that,' I said. One of the trainers who had helped me off then had an idea. 'Will it only get ruptured if it goes back in again?'

'Well, yes,' said the doc.

'Well, why don't we strap them?'

'Can it be done?' says the coach. The doc nodded. I then stood up, the doc grabbed the green insulation tape that we always used to keep our socks up, held my two goolies together and wrapped the tape around the tubes above, so it was impossible for my nuts to go back up. A pain-killing injection, new shorts and shirt and off I trotted.

I managed to finish the game but have never been in such pain in my life. Probably the funniest part of the story though, was when the rest of the boys were showering and getting ready to get off to the club to have a few beers, there was I, razor blade in hand, one hair by one, cutting the tape off my knackers.

I have never complained about ripping off an Elastoplast since!

* * *

I was captain of a team in England in the 1960s, and we had a prop forward who had never scored a try in his career. I thought that this was slightly tough, so I devised a move in training that would ensure that he got hold of the ball at the crucial moment, five yards out, and he could then barge his way over. He was massive, 19 or 20 stone. 'No one will stop you,' I said.

So the match was in full flow, we were leading quite comfortably, and so I called the move. 'Are you sure?' he said.

'Yes, of course,' and called the move again: 'Roly Poly.' I shouted.

It worked a treat. Over he dived. TRY! I ran over to congratulate him.

'Do not touch me,' he said, 'Just do not touch me.' The paramedics came on, were very careful and it took seven of them to roll this 20-stone prop onto the stretcher. The crowd were very subdued, we all thought he had done his spine in or broken his neck. Everyone was hugely concerned. Anyway the match continued and as soon as the half-time whistle blew, being captain, I raced down the tunnel to see how he was.

I ran into the medics' room and saw the doc.

'How is he?' I asked.

'F***ing how is he? He can f***ing tell you how he is. I have never been so embarrassed in my life.'

'What do you mean?'

'Go and ask the bastard. We held the game up for seven minutes, I was really worried that he had broken his back, we carried the great lump into the medical room, gently put him down, and he hops off the stretcher, shakes his leg and drops a seven-pounder onto the floor.'

In the excitement of scoring the first try in his career he had shat himself. I went in to see him.

'What the f*** were you doing?' I asked.

'Well, this was the only thing I could do, I wasn't going to stand up in front of players and the crowd and shake it out there, I had to get in here and drop it onto the floor here.'

True story – the player though, shall remain anonymous.

An England international cricketer and former captain, he has played in 121 Test matches, scored 7,896 runs at an average of over 40 and made 15 centuries. No man has played more Test matches for England. While playing behind the stumps for England he has 155 Test dismissals to his name. Stewart plays his first-class cricket for Surrey and has hit over 25,000 runs. He has been one of English cricket's finest servants, and still continues to play a vital role in the country's fortunes.

During the 1996–97 tour of Zimbabwe, England left-arm seamer Alan Mullally was asked in a TV interview how he would occupy his time away from cricket.

'Ah, I'm not much of a Tommy tourist, mate,' he replied. 'So I guess I'll just go down the beach, catch a few rays and do a bit of surfing.'

Good effort Al, Zimbabwe is landlocked in the middle of Africa!

A Scotland rugby union international prop who made his debut in 1996 v Italy. He has won 33 caps to date and plays his club rugby for Northampton Saints.

During the Six Nations Rugby Championships, at the Calcutta Cup match, there is a lightning strike and it tragically kills both Clive Woodward and Ian McGeechan instantly.

They both ascend into heaven and are met at the Pearly Gates by the Boss himself.

'Welcome, gentlemen,' says God. 'Come on in. I'll show you your accommodation.'

He takes Clive by the hand, and leads him off on a short walk through beautiful fields of flowers until they come across a pretty thatched cottage by a stream, with a well-laid-out garden, lovely flower beds and tall trees gently swaying in the breeze.

The thatched roof forms the shape of St George's Cross, the birds in the trees are whistling 'Swing Low, Sweet Chariot,' and the gnomes by the garden path are images of great English rugby heroes, past and present: David Duckham, Bill Beaumont, Jason Leonard, and his old mate Lawrence Dallaglio.

'Gosh,' says Clive, 'I don't know what to say.'

God smiles at him, takes Ian McGeechan by the hand and starts to walk up the path.

As they are strolling away, Clive looks around him and, a little farther up the road, he sees a gigantic mansion, with massive pillars carved like thistles, Scottish lions on the gates and fields of heather all around.

The house and gardens are surrounded by stands of Scots pine and Douglas fir. On the lawns, there are huge 20ft golden statues of Andy Irvine, Roy Laidlaw, Finlay Calder and the two Hastings brothers, overlooking a beautiful, magnificent garden.

Massed choirs of birds are singing 'Flower of Scotland', tenor and bass in perfect harmony.

Slightly concerned, Clive runs after God and Ian McGeechan and, tapping God on the shoulder, says:

'Excuse me God, I don't wish to sound ungrateful or anything, but I was wondering why Ian's house is, well, you know, so much bigger and even more grand than mine.'

God laughs, puts a consoling arm around Clive's shoulder and says to him softly:

'There, there, Clive, don't worry, it's not Ian's house. It's mine!'

STUART STOREY

A member of Great Britain's 1968 Olympic athletics team, he has been an athletics commentator since 1973.

As an athletics commentator with BBC television for the last 30 years, I've covered seven Olympic Games. After my first three Olympic games I went back to my old rugby club, Upper Clapton Rugby Club in Epping to play for the 'Golden Oldies' for charity. Many of my team-mates from the original first team were playing and assembled in the bar after the game. Now, my face is seldom, if ever, seen on the television screen so I can excuse most people for not recognising me.

A young man at the club approached me and asked me for a pound for my match fee.

'Great,' I said. He then mentioned that I'd played quite well and why didn't I play regularly on a Saturday.

'Because,' I said, 'I'm in television.'

'Oh,' he said, 'that's good, give me your name and address, I didn't know you could get repairs done on a Saturday.'

* * *

I got the *Daily Telegraph Faux Pas* award for my commentary of the Los Angeles Olympics men's high jump competition in 1984.

'Zhu JIANHUA of China, the tallest high jumper in the world and holder of the record has had an early failure in this Olympic High Jump final .... Remember back one year to those wonderful inaugural World Athletics Championships in Helsinki when exactly the same thing happened. Once again it looks as though it will have cost him the gold medal ... there is quite clearly a chink in his armour!!!'

WALTER SWINBURN

Currently a racing commentator for Channel 4, the former jockey notched up 1,391 career wins in the UK. Perhaps his most famous came in the 1981 Derby where, riding Shergar, he won by a record 10 lengths. He also rode Shergar to success in the Arc de Triomphe in the same year.

One of my favourite racing tales comes from 1960 in Calcutta, India. My father, Wally Swinburn, had just won the Queen Elizabeth Cup on a horse called Pa Bear. Her Majesty the Queen was at the racecourse and was to present the trophy to the happy owners, Mr and Mrs Billmoria. On receiving the trophy an ecstatic Mr Billmoria said to the Queen, 'Thank you, Mrs Queen, from the bottom of my heart, and also from my wife's bottom!'

Years later at a lunch with the Queen, I reminded her of the occasion and we both had a good laugh about it.

✳   ✳   ✳

As a young jockey I needed to shed a few pounds to ride in a race in Italy. As a last resort I took the diuretics offered to me by

254

Greville Starkey, who assured me that I would get rid of the excess pounds in liquid form during our flight. Imagine my horror and discomfort once I boarded the plane – it was a small jet and there was no toilet. The more I wriggled in my seat the more Greville and Pat Eddery giggled. Eventually I found a plastic vase under my seat – heaven sent – and with apologies to the ladies on board I relieved myself. I never took another diuretic!

T

JOHNNY TAPIA

_The current Featherweight world champion and former
world Super Flyweight champion._

We've all got a story to tell. My dad was shot dead before I was
born. My mother was kidnapped when I was seven, assaulted,
raped, hung, and stabbed with an ice pick 22 times. When I was
eight, I was in a bus that went 80 feet over a cliff and people
died all around me. I've been in jail for robbery and cocaine.
I've been clinically dead three times. God knows why I'm here.
My wife Theresa has saved me. She's the only person in the
world I trust. If she left me, you guys had better watch out.

Theresa Tapia on her husband:
Johnny can't go out on his own. He'll do something to someone, probably himself. I watch him 24/7. The reason for this is
that when Johnny was being read his last rites after obscene
cocaine abuse, having been clinically dead for a minute and 23
seconds, my world was over. Amazingly, he came round. I took
him home and sat with him all night. But I fell asleep. When I
woke up Johnny was gone. I searched the house, then called

the police. They found him in a nightclub. He'd gone out the night he'd died. He said, 'Baby, I had to go out. I have never taken my eyes off him again.

BOB TAYLOR

———— • ◆ • ————

An England international cricketer between 1970 and 1983, he won 57 Test caps. He took 1,473 catches and made 176 stumpings for Derbyshire.

It was the England tour to Australia in 1974–75. Tourists always have practical jokers in the party, and in our case it was David Lloyd and Mike Hendrick. They used to buy exploding cigarettes, stink bombs and the like. On one occasion the team were about to depart the then brand new Melbourne airport to fly to Sydney.

The tour party were sitting in a group in the terminal lounge, waiting for our flight call, when David Lloyd suddenly produced a very realistic 'curly wurly' dog mess. He then put it on the terminal floor just in front of the group.

For the next 20 minutes or so it was hilarious watching the Aussie passengers tripping over and pulling funny faces at the sight of what looked like the real thing. Just then we saw an attendant with his little brush and shovel, he bent down to brush it onto his shovel, when David Lloyd got up and put it in his pocket. The look on this bloke's face would have been ideal for 'Candid Camera!'

* * *

Again in Australia, my first tour, in 1970–71. Alan Knott was the no. 1 keeper so I was assigned to do twelfth-man duties. It was the final day of the inaugural Test match in Perth. The game was heading for a draw, the Aussies were fielding, and I was taking drinks out with the Aussie twelfth man (no buggies in those days).

The Aussies were playing for time, the umpires were telling the two of us to leave the field.

To my total embarrassment, the tray of empty glasses fell to the ground with me left with just the handles in my hand. I got a lot of 'Pommy this' and 'Pommy that' from the crowd.

I soon found out who the practical joker was who had partly detached one of the handles.

When we went out with the next drinks, I doctored his with 'Andrews Liver Salts' and for the rest of the day he was on and off the field heading for the nearest loo. I think I got my own back!

DENNIS TAYLOR

The 1985 World Snooker champion, beating Steve Davis in the last frame of the final, potting the last black. It was reported that almost half the population of the country was watching, live on the BBC, as he sank the final ball to claim the title. It is one of the most famous moments in the history of the sport.

My uncle Seamus went up in a two-seater plane with his best friend Pat. He shouted to Pat:

'If we fly this plane upside down, will we fall out?'

Pat shouted back:

'Don't be stupid, we will still be friends.'

* * *

My uncle Seamus can't understand why he only has one brother and his sister has two.

GRAHAM TAYLOR

*A former footballer for Grimsby Town and Lincoln City,
Taylor took up management and held the reigns at Lincoln
and twice at Watford where he led them to the Cup Final in
1984. He then managed Wolves and is now at Aston Villa
for the second time. He is perhaps best known though, as the
man in charge of England between 1990 and 1993. His
tenure came to an end when he resigned after England
failed to qualify for the 1994 World Cup.*

When I was a player at Grimsby Town in my very early years, the manager was giving a team talk when he suddenly stopped, put a finger to his lips to quieten everyone, tiptoed to the door of the dressing room, pulled it open and a director, who had been crouched listening behind the door, fell through.

The manager walked out and left the director with the players. He told us he had dropped his watch and had been looking for it. What a porky-pie!!

* * *

I was a player at Lincoln City. One day we all came in from training, got bathed and dressed. When we tried to get our shoes on we couldn't. Some prankster had nailed our shoes to the wooden dressing room floor – seems funny now – but it wasn't then.

We all suspected who the person was, but to this day no one is really sure. Was it the chairman or the manager because we had been on a losing run?

*A former Wales rugby union international and a Lions
tourist in 1968 and 1971. Unusually for a flanker, he was
the chosen international place kicker. He is now the ITV
lead rugby union commentator.*

Circa 1975, Wales decided on a signal at set scrums to tell the
forwards which way the backs intended to move the ball so
that the support players knew exactly where to go. The two
flankers were Trevor Evans from Swansea and Terry Cobner
from Pontypool. They packed down left and right rather than
open and blind so, to keep things simple for the front row, it
was agreed that any word beginning with 'S' for Swansea
would mean the move was going left whilst an initial 'P' would
indicate right.

Eventually, confident that everybody understood, it was
time to take the new ploy on to the practice field and Gareth
Edwards was the man to make the call just before he put-in the
ball. What did he shout?

'PSYCHOLOGY!'

The Pontypool front row went left, the rest of the forwards
went right and another good idea bit the dust!

* * *

Steve Smith and I were commentating on one of the worst
games of rugby I have ever seen – the 3rd/4th place play-off
between England and France (which neither side wanted to
play) at the 1995 World Cup.

Suddenly, there was a moment of excitement. The director
whispered into my ear the momentous news that John Major
had resigned as leader of the Conservative Party. I immediately
put on my state occasion voice and told the nation, explaining
that we would be staying with the match but would be going

to ITN's John Suchet on the final whistle for all the details. Quick as a flash, in came Smithy: 'Well, I know it's bad John, but surely there's no need for the Prime Minister to resign over a game of rugby.'

MARK TAYLOR

———————◆———————

A Wales rugby union international and British Lions tourist in 2001.

Dai from Tumble was having a spot of bother with his wife. She kept complaining about his obsession with tractors, and how she felt they were more important to him than their marriage. She did have a point: the back garden was full of broken down tractors – John Deere, Massey Ferguson, the lot. Anyway, it reached breaking point when a delivery of tractor gearboxes and clutches arrived one morning.

'That's it,' said the wife. 'Either the tractors go or I go.'

Dai thought long and hard about this, but eventually decided that he loved his wife more than the tractors, so he got rid of the lot.

A week later, Dai is walking through Tumble very despondently. Suddenly, he hears a woman screaming for help.

'Help! Come quick! My house is on fire!' Quick as a flash, Dai runs to the house, opens the door, takes a deep breath and blows as hard as he can. The flames are blown out instantly.

'That was amazing', said the woman. 'How did you do it?'

'Well,' said Dai, 'I'm an ex-tractor fan!'

* * *

A panda is walking down the street when he bumps into a prostitute.

'Fancy a quickie?' asks the woman.

'Why not,' says the panda. So they go to the prostitute's flat and have great sex. When it's all over, the panda gets up to leave. The woman stops him.

'Where do you think you're going?' she asks.

'Home,' says the panda.

'But I want paying,' says the woman.

'Why?' asks the panda.

'Because I'm a prostitute,' says the woman. The panda is confused by this.

'What's a prostitute?' he asks. The woman throws him a dictionary. The panda looks up 'prostitute' and sees the definition, 'a woman who performs sexual favours in return for money.'

The panda throws the dictionary back to the woman as he walks out of the door, telling her to look up the definition of 'panda'. She does. It reads, 'Panda – eats shoots and leaves.'

PETER TAYLOR

An England football international who played for Southend United, Crystal Palace, Tottenham Hotspur, Leyton Orient and Oldham Athletic. The former winger then went on to manage Southend, the England Under 21 team, Gillingham, Leicester City and Brighton. He was also appointed caretaker manager of the full England side in November 2000 for games against Italy and Spain.

After we had been put out of the 1998 World Cup, when David Batty missed that penalty, we were all waiting to board the bus to take us to the airport to fly back to base.

I was talking when we saw Michelle Farrer, who was Glenn Hoddle's secretary, crying her eyes out, when David said to me, 'What penalty did she miss?'

* * *

When I was 17 years of age, just starting a pro career, I got sent off playing for Southend Reserves against Brighton Reserves.

I was actually fouled and pushed the player away. He got booked and I got sent off, to everybody's amazement. The manager slaughtered me, but after the game we found the referee's name was Peter Taylor. He thought I was taking the rise out of him when I was asked for my name. I was eventually let off.

DAVE THOMAS

A former England international footballer, he played for Burnley, QPR, Everton, Wolverhampton Wanderers, Vancouver Whitecaps, Middlesbrough and Portsmouth.

On a mid-season break in Majorca, staying in an exclusive hotel, we were all having dinner. The manager asked the physio what he was eating.

The physio replied, 'Welsh rarebit.'

To which the manager responded in a loud voice, 'Bloody hell, it looks like cheese on toast to me!'

'Laughter can be more satisfying than honour; more precious than money; more heart-cleansing than prayer.'

Harriet Rochlin

Laughter is like the human body wagging its tail.

DEREK THOMPSON

An ex-amateur jockey and top show jumper, Thompson's proudest moment came when he beat the Prince of Wales in a flat race at Plumpton in 1981. He worked as an assistant trainer to Denys Smith and with Pierre Sanoner in Chantilly, and is now a broadcaster for the Channel 4 racing team.

We had just shown a feature on a female masseuse who helped injured jockeys make a quick recovery and get back into the saddle. My colleague John McCririck asked:

'What is so good about this particular masseuse?'

I replied without thinking:

'The beauty of this girl is that she will drop anything for a jockey!'

Big Mac fell about, and realising what I'd said, I did too but hoped that the masseuse, Val Ridgeway, didn't take it too literally!

* * *

My wife Julie was judging the best-dressed lady at the races. She'd picked the 1-2-3 but then my colleague, John Francome, suggested that I ask her about her outfit, which I did.

'Well,' came the reply, 'it's the same one as the outfit I had on last year, because you are too tight to buy me a new one!'

I am still asked to this day whether I have bought my wife a new outfit yet.

265

ANDREW THORNTON

—— • ◆ • ——

A National Hunt jockey, who has won both the Cheltenham
Gold Cup and the Scottish Grand National.

At Leicester there are 20 or so people watching racing in the weighing room, as usual. Sophie Mitchell (one of the few lady jockeys) is sitting on a table with ten or so male jockeys watching the racing – the other ten are behind the table. Jamie Osbourne (now training) is standing behind her and starts stroking her ear and neck and basically just having a bit of fun. He then turns round to light a fag. In the meantime, Sophie moves and Eugine Husband (a fellow jockey) moves along the table to where Sophie was sitting. Jamie continues to stroke what he thinks is Sophie's neck and ear.

He gets the shock of his life when Eugine turns around and says:

'What the f*** do you think you're doing, get off me!'

You should've heard the roar from everyone who saw it!

BILL THRELFALL

—— • ◆ • ——

A tennis broadcaster for 36 years, Threlfall has
commentated on all the major competitions across the
world. The former Fleet Air Arm pilot has been a BBC com-
mentator for 28 years. He switched to television in 1974,
and has been a regular commentator at the Wimbledon
Championships ever since. As a player, Bill won a record
eight Royal Navy titles.

I was sitting in a night-club in the early 1960s, while in the Fleet Air Arm, on a table hosted by Aristotle Onassis. To my astonishment, when I arrived who should be there but

Winston Churchill, his wife, Margot Fontaine and other notables.

I felt totally out of my depth. As the evening progressed Lady Churchill felt a little sorry for me, and said:

'You know you must go and speak to the old man. He's sitting over there.'

He was a little deaf by this time. I wondered what on earth I could say. Having already had a wonderful dance with Lady Churchill, and rather wanting another one, I thought out of courtesy to ask his permission this time. I went over to the now-hard of hearing Churchill himself and said, 'Could I have the pleasure of having a dance with your wife?'

'Could you have the pleasure of giving me the dance of my life?' he replied. 'Certainly not, I don't dance, not with men anyway.'

*   *   *

I was commentating with Peter West: 'Bjorn Borg, the top wanking Swede.'

MIKE TINDALL

An England rugby union international, the hard-running centre made his debut v Ireland in 2000 and has won 18 caps to date.

A man goes to see the doctor.

'Sorry to bother you, Doc, but I seem to have a problem getting it up.'

'No problem,' says the doctor, 'I will give you some pioneering surgery. I can take the muscle from an elephant's trunk and fit it into your penis and you'll never struggle again.'

The man has no hesitation: 'Fix me up, Doc.'

So he has the operation, no problems – all is great. The day comes for his first date. Candles, fine wine, a beautiful woman across the table, all is perfect ….

The man's trousers then start to stir as he begins to get a little aroused. He feels his penis growing and growing. Suddenly it breaks through his trousers, grabs the bread from the table then disappears.

The woman sees this, and with a twinkle in her eye and a smile forming on her lips asks, 'Can you do that again?'

'Sure,' replies the man, 'but I don't think that I can fit another bread roll up my arse!'

* * *

A naval boiler stoker goes to Hell. The Devil comes up to him on the first day and sees him smiling.

'What are you so happy about?' says Lucifer.

'I just love it here. It's like a spring day in the boiler-room.'

The Devil walks off angry, and decides to get him.

'I'll turn the heat all the way up. That'll show him.'

The next day, the Devil checks back with our hero, only to find him happy once again.

'What now?' says the Evil One. 'This heat is great! Reminds me of a summer day in the boiler-room.'

The Devil realises that he has been going about it all wrong.

'Tomorrow I'm going to make it colder than a Siberian winter.'

He returns the next day to find the stoker shivering and blue, but grinning from ear to ear.

'What could you possibly have to be happy about?'

'It's pretty obvious, isn't it?' replied the stoker. 'Manchester City must have won the Premier League!'

Dan has enjoyed a long and illustrious career as an oarsman and rowing coach. He coached Oxford through their longest-ever victorious sequence in the Oxford-Cambridge Boat Race between 1976 and 1986.

When I was training with my doubles partner for the World Rowing Championships in 1978, we were invited by the world's leading coach, Thor Neilsen, to spend two weeks racing under his tutorship with the Spanish and Russian teams in Banyoles – later site of the 1992 Olympic course.

After six days of three daily sessions, Neilsen had said nothing – just scrutinising from a launch moored at the mid-way point on the training lake, taking copious notes. Finally we approached the great man for his thoughts on our progress.

'Thor, it's great here, very valuable, but we wondered if you had any tips?'

'Well,' he said slowly, 'if you put your oars', and he demonstrated carefully with his hand, explaining seriously, 'more quickly into the water', he made a chopping motion, 'and you pull your sculls more harder through the water', all said with a slow Scandinavian accent, 'I think you will go faster'.

That was it! Two weeks of coaching. The clue? Keep it simple.

ANDY TOWNSEND

—◆—

*A Republic of Ireland international footballer, he has
captained his country and also played for Southampton,
Norwich City, Chelsea, Aston Villa and Middlesbrough. He
is now an ITV football analyst.*

After the World Cup in 1990 my wife and I spent a few days in
Dublin chilling out. Everywhere we went, people were asking
for photos and autographs and shaking my hand. Eventually
we decided to get out of the main shopping area and headed
off to find a bar.

While walking down this little side road I noticed a woman
across the road with a camera. Without hesitation I stopped,
adopted a sickly smile and posed for the camera thinking,
'Get on with it, Love'. After a few seconds of waiting, the
woman suddenly said:

'Will ye get out off the f***ing way!'

I turned round and to my horror (and my wife's delight)
there was a beautiful statue behind me and this woman was
trying to take a photo of that!

GREGOR TOWNSEND

—◆—

*A Scotland rugby union international who is the most
capped Scot in the history of the game with 66 caps to date.
He was also a Lions tourist in 1997.*

It was 1995, an emotional day. Scotland had just beaten France
in Paris for the first time in 30 years. Gavin Hastings had
sprinted in for a 40 m try under the posts to clinch victory. We
were getting stuck into the evening in a big way.

The French were, of course, hosting and we were having

dinner in a beautiful banquet room – chandeliers, the lot.

When we were served our main course the dinner plates were too hot to touch – piping hot. Someone discovered that if you tapped them firmly with a spoon they would shatter. Well, this was an open invitation to have some fun.

Everyone was leaning over, trying to smash everyone else's plate and, to a large extent, succeeding. We weren't too bothered, we were going crazy, had just won and were on the piss in a major way.

The food was eventually cleared away and it was time for the captains' speeches. What would Gavin Hastings say, having just scored a crucial try that had broken French hearts? What was he going to say that would show how magnanimous in victory he and his team were?

He hit upon the idea that in order to show due respect to the wonderful hosts, he would say a word or two in French; the only problem was, Gavin couldn't speak a word of the language. No problem, Damian Cronin, who had spent a season or two in France and who could obviously speak the language, helped him out.

Gavin Hastings stood up, all the attending guests became quiet. The man that typified Scottish rugby, who was not only an idol to many but also a true ambassador for the game and Scotland itself, looked at his notes and started his speech. He asked Cronin to translate:

'Dear ladies and gentlemen, it gives me great pleasure to stand before you. I thank you for your kind hospitality, after a mad, passionate game.'

At the end of the first sentence the French section of the audience erupted, cheering and clapping, Hastings was a huge hit.

Our ambassador, although a little surprised at the French response to what he thought was a fairly standard opening few lines, smiled broadly and milked the clapping, in blissful ignorance.

What had Cronin actually translated for him?

'Dear Ladies & Gentleman, it gives me great pleasure to tell you that as soon as I finish this speech I am looking forward to taking my wife upstairs and having mad, passionate sex with her!'

The French loved it!

TIM TREMLETT

————— ◆ —————

A Hampshire cricketer between 1976 and 1991, he played for England B in Sri Lanka in 1986 and is now Director of Cricket for Hampshire.

One of my first County Championship matches was played against Yorkshire at Southampton in 1978.

I scratched around terribly when batting and kept edging Arnie Sidebottom just short or through the slips. Arnie kept clutching his head and was tearing his hair out when, finally, he screamed at me, ' You lucky ******!!'

The umpire, David Constant, immediately called the Yorkshire captain, Geoffrey Boycott over.

'Excuse me, Geoff, but your fast bowler cannot speak to a batsman like that.'

Geoff glared at me, then Arnie, before acknowledging the umpire. 'Let me get this straight, my bowler said the batsman is a "lucky ******!!"'

'Yes,' replied the umpire.

'But he's not allowed to say it to his face,' says Geoff.

'Correct,' says Constant.

'Okay, what if he *thinks* he is a lucky ******!!'

'That's fine,' says Constant.

Geoff turned slowly towards me, grinned and out loud said, 'Tremlett, my bowler thinks you are a lucky ******!!'

MERIEL TUFNELL

―――――――― • ◆ • ――――――――

The first ever licensed female Flat Racing jockey under
Jockey Club Rules. In 1972 she was the first woman to
become the Champion Jockey, was Reserve Champion in
1973 and European Champion in 1974 (still the only
British winner). Meriel founded and chaired the only ever
Lady Jockeys' Association in 1972, which represented
women in Britain, Europe, USA, and Australia before it
merged with the Men's Association in 1997.

In my riding days abroad, we had what we called the international BUT.

For instance, on arriving in Denmark to ride, I was met by the
trainer who said, 'Ah! You are ze Ingush girl, ya?'
   'Yes.'
   'Vell, I av a wery nice orz for you to ride BUTT e az to av
(how you zay?) Blindts?'
   'Blindfolds.'
   'Ya! BUTT you muzed not take zem off until afder ze gates
ofen!'
   On arriving at the start, the German champion (Mikel Smit)
took over the situation and explained all to the starter. Taking a
quick glance towards me, the starter said, 'Don't look zo vor-
ried Miss Toofnell, it will be alwight az long az you pull zem
off befooor you reach ze bendt!!'

Then, on arriving in Sweden to ride I was met again by the
trainer who said, 'Ah! you are ze Inglish girl, ya?'
   'Yes.'
   'Vell I av a wery nice orz for you to ride BUTT e iz wery tem-
premental and gets frite vith ze niose off ze crowd, zo I putz ze

cotton vool in iz eers and you pulls ze plugs out in ze startz. Ze noise of ze people vill zen make im run vaster.'

Once on top of the horse, I realised what the cotton wool was with great amusement. The horse had two tampax jammed into his ears, with a tape running between the two, behind his ears! This was for me to get hold of and pull out as we reached the crowd!

Neither of these situations would be allowed under our Jockey Club Rules.

PHIL TUFNELL

———————— •◆• ————————

An England international cricketer, who took 121 Test wickets with his slow left-arm spin, and has taken over 1,000 first-class wickets. He is nicknamed 'The Cat'.

I have to admit that over the years I have managed to get myself in the odd spot of bother. Apparently my attitude has not been quite what various selectors and captains have looked for in their left-arm spinner.

My off-the-field lifestyle has also led to one or two misunderstandings, most notably in New Zealand where I unwittingly became the focus for a publicity campaign for a winebar in Christchurch.

I woke one morning to find myself plastered all over the front of the local paper for apparently having smoked grass in the gents at an establishment called Bardelli's. By ten o'clock that same morning a rash of posters appeared around town declaring, 'Tufnell reckons that Bardelli's is the best joint in town.'

It was complete nonsense, of course. I was invisible at the time.

A Somerset wicketkeeper-batsman who has also played for England A.

I phoned my wife in England from New Zealand while on a cricket tour to wish her Happy Birthday. After I completed my tuneful chorus of 'Happy Birthday to You' there followed a moment's silence before the voice said, 'That's very nice but I've no idea who you are.' I had the wrong number. What made it worse was that I had actually forgotten my home number and had to call international directory enquires to ensure I got the right one!

* * *

I was batting with Pakistani Test cricketer Mushtaq Ahmed. Mushtaq hit the ball into the outfield and called to run. The bowler made some comment as Mushtaq ran past, along the lines of it being a lucky shot and he should have been out. Mushtaq took exception and, whilst making the second run, he was still arguing with the bowler, waving his bat and actually running backwards. Not realising this, I called him through for an easy third run, or so I thought. Mushtaq had lost a lot of ground and had no chance of recovering it – he was run out by about three yards. Mushtaq was still waving his bat at the bowler all the way back to the pavilion.

U

RORY UNDERWOOD

A former England rugby union winger, he is the second highest international try scorer of all time with 49 tries. He is England's top try scorer and was a Lions tourist in 1989 and 1993. He played his club rugby for Leicester between 1983 and 1997, making over 230 appearances.

On a mid-week match against South Australia during the 1988 England tour of Australia, the RFU committee were highly embarrassed and angry that the England rugby team were not on the pitch, lined up and singing the National Anthem.

Why?

Nigel 'Ollie' Redman's routine was to visit the toilet just before going onto the pitch. Unfortunately a combination of Ollie mis-timing his pit stop and the zeal of the Bandmaster created a scenario where we were just about to walk down the tunnel when the England manager Geoff Cooke stopped us just in time. We could hear the first notes of 'God Save the Queen'.

* * *

277

Mark Regan's nickname when he first joined the England squad was 'Lightning'.

Why? When he was throwing into the line-out, he never hit the same spot twice.

V

BRAAM VAN STRAATEN
─────── •◆• ───────

*A former South African rugby union international, he is the
fourth highest Springbok points scorer in the history of the
game with 221 points in 21 Tests.*

I have never been a drinker and never will be; in fact I am tee-
total but there was one occasion when I succumbed.

I was playing for the world-famous Barbarians team and we
were due to take on Wales at the Millennium Stadium – a huge
fixture. However, as is the tradition of the club, we did not
train obsessively and managed to take time off during the
week. It was Thursday, and a few of us had just finished playing golf at a very famous golf club in Wales. The players? Me,
Joost van der Westhuizen, Robin Brooke, John Langford and
Tim Horan among others.

We were in the bar, having a natter, all the boys with their
beer, me with my orange juice and lemonade when Tim Horan
mentioned that it was his birthday. Any excuse for a celebration – more drinks were ordered and the boys started piling in.
Tim, though, was not happy that I was not on the beers so
every time he saw a soft drink, he crushed a packet of crisps

and emptied them in. Before I knew it I had a Guinness in my hand and was on the piss with the rest of them. Drinking games then started up – 'Spoof' and others, and we began to get well oiled.

The President of the Golf Club came over and announced:

'You are playing for the Barbarians, the ultimate team. You are guests of ours and can't do anything wrong here.'

That was an error. The President wandered off. Tim Horan jumps up to test his offer, drops his trousers and waddles around this prestigious golf club, no reaction from any officials – we were in hysterics.

John Langford then disappeared, only to return wearing purple – not normal purple though: a woman's purple tracksuit. Where he got it from I don't know – it was skin tight, far too small and stretched across his huge fame; he sat down and continued to drink.

The Chairman then brought in cigars. Things were warming up nicely. I was all over the place, not being a drinker. The bar then shut and so we ordered a taxi. We were waiting outside patiently, Langford still in his woman's tracksuit, when the 18th green was spotted ...

Off we sprinted, across the dew-soaked grass and onto the green, in unison we all dived full-length onto this perfectly manicured turf, the victory slide now complete.

Horan was mucking about on the edge of the 18th, just above a deep bunker, which was 3 ft below. Only one thing for it, I ploughed into Horan, it is always great to floor a Wallaby, on the pitch, or rolling about in a bunker ....

One member of our party had by now, passed out by the hole. We missed the team dinner, the coach, Bob Dwyer, was not happy, but hey, it's not every day that I get on the beers. In fact that was the last time, but what a belter ....

*A sports presenter and commentator who was for many years
the face and voice of the BBC's* Ski Sunday, *as well as show
jumping and snooker.*

I arrived one morning at the Hickstead show jumping ground
to present 'The Derby' on television. I was still suffering from a
bit of a party the night before and wandered down to the
sponsor's caravan for a pick-me-up.

On the way a charming young lady, yet to reach her teens,
waved a programme in front of me and said:

'Will you..?'

Out came the Vine pen and an autograph was given. As I
walked away, I looked back and she was staring, rather puz-
zled, at the programme.

'Is that OK?' I said.

'You've gone and scribbled all over it so you'll have to buy it,'
she replied. 'I'm selling programmes!'

'Inside Track' of the *Sunday Times* ran the story: 'Vine pays £2
for his own autograph.'

W

SID WADDELL

*A darts broadcaster who won the All-Yorkshire Shove
Ha'penny Championship in 1971, the Fleet Street Pro-Am
Pairs Darts Championship (with Eric Bristow) in 1981 and
was named the Sports Commentator of the Year in 2001.*

In 1978, the British Darts Organisation introduced very strict
dress codes for televised matches. No 'jeans-type trouser' could
be worn. In 1980 I was sitting in the commentary box ready to
go live on 'Grandstand' when a scuffle broke out off-stage. One
of the semi-finalists in the British Open, a milkman from the
West Country, had come on to the oche wearing jeans.

Officials dragged him off and de-trousered him. With a BBC
floor manager screaming at him, the milkman, who was about
5'4" tall, borrowed the trousers off his pal who was 6'2". The
waist was many inches too big so he played the game holding
up the trousers with his left hand. He lost.

* * *

I get totally absorbed when I commentate on darts and my
nose gets ever nearer the monitor screens as a game goes on. At

such times, I've also been known to drink water from the jug rather than the glass. At a tournament in Middlesbrough, Les (our new floor manager and a bit of a wag) noticed this and, in the middle of an exciting game, I grabbed the jug, tipped it … and noticed two fat goldfish swimming round.

'Time to report to the funny farm,' I thought, 'you've flipped.' Les had bought them from the local market. Another inch and the *Sun* could have reported, 'SID WADDELL DRANK MY GOLDFISH.'

"Where's the umpire? I want to appeal against the light!"

ROB WAINWRIGHT

A former Scotland rugby union international, winning 37 caps, 16 of them as captain. He was a Lions tourist in 1997.

In the lead-up to any game, the coaches have their say in the hour before kick-off, the players warm up and maybe practise a couple of line-outs and run-throughs. But, as kick-off approaches, the focus is on the captain. With a couple of minutes left 'til kick-off, his words can add the final touches to the team's preparation.

There is the apocryphal tale of one captain's final words to his team. The team is in a huddle in the changing room, a minute before kick-off. The skipper is on one knee in the centre of the huddle, inspiring his team.

'There are two things to remember today, men! Firstly, there is going to be only one team out there today. How many teams will there be out there, then lads?'

'ONE TEAM!' came the resounding reply.

'Secondly, just remember this. It is going to be a case of our team being 'men v boys,' OK?'

'ONE TEAM, MEN VERSUS BOYS!' chant the team. At that moment, the ref puts his head round the changing-room door and calls, 'Right boys, let's be having you, time to go!'

PETER WALKER

A former England international cricketer, he also played for Glamorgan, scored 17,650 runs and took 834 wickets. He was a superb close fielder and held 656 catches for his county.

When playing for Glamorgan against Northamptonshire at Ebbw Vale, a Welsh valley town, I went to tap down a divot on the very wet pitch. To this day I'm absolutely certain I heard a tapping back from below ground – presumably a miner on shift!

* * *

Lubbe Snoyman was a legendary umpire in the Transvaal cricket league. While umpiring a match on a ground adjacent to another, a huge appeal went up from nearby, at exactly the same time as the batsman in the game he was umpiring played and missed the ball.

Without a moment's hesitation Lubbe gave the batsman in his game out and refused to listen to any protests from the departing batsman!

JIM WATT

—◆—

A successful amateur, he turned professional in 1968, winning the British Lightweight championship on two separate occasions. Watt was also European Lightweight champion from 1977 to 1979 and went on to become World Lightweight Champion between 1979 and 1981. He retired having won 38 of his 48 professional fights. He is now a commentator on the sport.

Reg Gutteridge and I were commentating on a European heavyweight fight in Denmark. The Danish boxer beat the Swedish one and the ring was invaded by fans dressed as vikings! Loads of them. Reg was climbing into the ring to do the interviews and, as always, I had to fill while he got himself into position. But he caught his wooden leg on a piece of metal on the corner. It was hysterical. I was trying not to laugh while talking over and over the same replay for about ten minutes! Reg was completely stuck and all these vikings were running round him ... then the ring collapsed and Reg was still trying to get the interview!

I'd been commentating on my own for what seemed ages and now I was struggling big time. I looked at Reg for help – he needed his own help – so, I turned to my producer and he looked blank.

He frantically scribbled something on a bit of paper and I thought, 'Thank God.'

He passed it to me and I read it. It said, 'Keep talking.'

That was when I knew why I was paid more to commentate than I was to fight!

JAN WEBSTER

A former England rugby union international.

On an England tour, this time to South Africa, the team decided on a day off to go to the top of Table Mountain in Cape Town. I've never really had a head for heights and on this particular occasion my worst fears were realised. Back in 1972, the cable car was not enclosed (although it did have safety bars). A certain Mike Burton thought what fun it would be to dangle a diminutive scrum half – myself – over the side. For those who have never experienced Table Mountain, most of its ascent is on a nice gradient. Then, all of a sudden, the last climb is a vertical cliff face and this is when my heart-stopping moment occurred. I believe I am the only one to have ever seen it upside down. Thanks, Mike.

Needless to say all the cable cars are now fully enclosed.

Mike Burton's profession now? A players' agent and travel tour boss.

PETER WEST

Most famous as a former BBC TV cricket commentator and presenter, he is also a former BBC radio rugby commentator.

I have always fancied the tale of Jim Laker asking Everton Weekes why he was so christened.

'Well,' said Everton, 'the year I was born Everton won the Championship.'

Jim, after some thought said, 'Bloody good job it wasn't West Bromwich Albion.'

* * *

Another favourite tale concerns Rex Alston, the distinguished BBC radio commentator whose obituary was prematurely published in *The Times*. Not many aspire to such a distinction. It is said that an outraged Rex telephoned *The Times* and demanded to be put through to the appropriate department.

'Obituaries here,' came a female voice.

'What the hell is going on?' Rex enquired. 'You have my obituary in the paper this morning and I'm still here, alive and kicking.'

There was a pregnant pause at one end of the line, followed by a nervous lady at the other end of the line. Finally, her splendid enquiry: 'Mr Alston, where are you speaking from?'

PETER WHEELER

An England rugby union international hooker between 1975 and 1984, winning 41 caps. He was a Lions tourist in 1977 and 1980 and is now Chief Executive at Leicester Tigers .

In the dressing room at Twickenham before the 1980 John Player Cup Final, I was endeavouring to wind the team up. I told them we had to use all the possession we had to its full advantage, but not to do anything silly, because if they tackled us early in the game and kicked the ball on to score, it would be a travesty. As I said that I just noticed our tight head prop, Steve Redfern, turn to a team mate and say, 'How many points will they get for a travesty?'

* * *

Moss Keane is in the dressing room having played for the British Lions in New Zealand in the game famous for the photograph of Fran Cotton in the mud. They had just won a tough provincial game narrowly in dreadful conditions. I asked Moss what the game was like.

He said, 'The first half was even and the second half even worse!'

CHRIS WHITE

———————— • ◆ • ————————

*A rugby union referee, White has taken charge of 18 inter-
nationals, including Six Nations, Tri Nations and World
Cup matches. He has refereed over 150 Premiership games.*

At the 1999 Mar del Plata 7s in Argentina, I was reffing the Argentina v France tie. The French were winning in front of 30,000 passionate home fans. A moat and a fence separated the pitch but we were in range of various fruits thrown by the crowd. The French captain went down injured in range of the crowd. I went to see him but was hit on my calf by a huge orange and had to be treated by a physio.

France went on to score a last-minute try to wrap up the game – right in the corner. The kicker and I walked back for the conversion right next to the moat, fence and crowd. A bar-rage of fruit rained down.

'Monsieur Arbite,' said the French kicker, 'what are you going to do about this?'

'I am going to stand in the middle of the pitch while you take the conversion,' I replied.

❉   ❉   ❉

It's the day before the crucial Rugby World Cup qualifier between Georgia, our excellent hosts, and their arch rivals, Russia, in Tblisi.

We were taken by our liaison officer to see a Royal Cathedral in the mountains above Tblisi. At the top of the cathedral was a stone hand.

'Why is that hand there?' I asked.

'Ah,' he said, 'that is the hand of the first mason who tried and failed to build the first cathedral.'

'Oh,' I replied. I thought for a moment and asked him, 'So what happens then to the referees who don't have good matches?' He looked me in the eye, smiled and said, 'Now you really understand Georgian humour!'

Georgia won 12–6 and the wine's not bad either.

JULIAN WHITE

An England rugby union international prop who made his debut in the famous 27–22 win over South Africa in Bloemfontein in 2000. White has won 13 caps.

An Englishman, a Scotsman and an Irishman are all to give speeches to the Deaf Association and are keen to give a good impression to their audience.

The Englishman goes first and, to the surprise of his colleagues, starts by rubbing his chest and then his groin. When he finishes, the Scotsman and Irishman asks him what he said.

'Well,' he explained, 'by rubbing my chest I indicated breasts, and thus ladies, and rubbing my groin I indicated balls and, thus, gentlemen. So my speech started – "Ladies and Gentlemen ..."'

On his way up to the podium the Scotsman thought to himself, 'I'll go one better than that bastard,' and started his speech by making an antler symbol with his fingers above his head while also rubbing his chest and groin. When he finished, his colleagues asked him what he had said.

'Well,' he explained, 'by imitating antlers and then rubbing my chest and groin I started the speech by saying – "Dear Ladies and Gentlemen ..."'

On his way up to the podium the Irishman thought to himself, 'I'll go even further than those two bastards,' and started his speech by making an antler symbol above his head, rubbing his chest and then his groin, and then masturbating furiously. When he finished, one of his colleagues asked him what he was doing.

'Well,' he explained, 'by imitating antlers, rubbing my chest, then my groin and masturbating I was starting my speech by saying – 'Dear Ladies and Gentlemen, it gives me great pleasure …"'

STEVE WILD

The English golfer turned professional aged 50 after a long career representing Staffordshire in amateur county golf. He now divides his time between the European Seniors Tour and running a successful industrial painting business.

A friend of mine was working in Wolverhampton at an engineering company, where the Sales Director passed away. Most of the staff wished to attend the funeral, so instead of all taking their own cars, it was decided to hire a coach for them all. The coach was ordered and on the due day it arrived.

Not until the coach was parked outside the offices did someone notice that the coach had been ordered from another Wolverhampton company and, spelled out in huge letters on the side were the words: "Happy Times"!

Masking tape was quickly used to obliterate the words.

291

An England rugby union international, the fly half has become one of the best goal-kickers the sport has ever seen. At 21 he became England's leading points scorer, smashing Rob Andrew's record of 396. He became England's youngest capped player for 71 years when he came on as a late replacement against Ireland in the 1998 Five Nations Championship, and has won 35 caps. He was a Lions tourist and is captain of the Newcastle Falcons.

A couple of years ago the Welsh team is playing England and just before kick-off the full back Shane Howarth slips, pulls a muscle and can't play. The coach Graham Henry is desperate as there aren't any other full backs in Wales, so he is forced to play a goose (it's OK though, it's got Welsh grandparents).

Rather surprisingly the goose has a brilliant first half. One minute it's clearing off its own line and making cover tackles, the next it's joined the line linking up perfectly with the backs. At half time Graham Henry is very pleased and everyone runs back onto the pitch for the second half.

On the way the ref starts chatting with the goose:

'Great first half mate, you must be really fit.'

'Thanks,' replied the goose, 'I try to keep myself fit but it's difficult finding the time so I try to do an hour in the gym each morning before work.'

'What do you do then?' asked the ref.

'I'm a chartered accountant,' replies the goose, at which point the ref immediately brandishes the red card and sends the goose off.

The bemused team-mates gather round the ref and start complaining.

'Sorry lads,' says the ref, 'I had no choice.'

'Professional fowl.'

BOB WILSON

A former Scotland international goalkeeper, he won the
European Fairs Cup and the Double with Arsenal in 1971.
He is now an ITV football presenter.

On an early appearance as presenter of BBC's 'Football Focus' in August 1974, having just retired as the Arsenal keeper, I was informed through my presenter's earpiece that Joe Jordan, who was not expected to be fit, had actually made it and was fit to play for Leeds United. I had approximately 30 seconds to decide how I would inform the nation, as we were on a video-tape item at the time. Early days in the new job and nerves resulted in the following when I reappeared in vision:

'Now before we move on, news just through from Elland Road that Joe Jordan has just pissed a late fatness test.'

* * *

The use of psychology in sport is important. The great Bill Shankly, Liverpool's legendary manager, was a master in unnerving the opposition. Just before one of my first games in the Arsenal first team, when I was a nervous amateur school-teacher just out of Loughborough University, he saw me placing tickets for my family at the players' entrance. Without showing he'd seen me, although I knew he had, and knowing how scared I was, he asked an Arsenal commissioner on the door, 'Excuse me, are Arsenal at full strength tonight, or is that Bob Wilson playing?'

You can imagine how (what little) confidence I had plummeted to a new low.

Y

SIR PETER YARRANTON

A former England rugby union international, a past President of the RFU, and Chairman of the UK Sports Council.

Mick Sullivan [formerly a Great Britain rugby league wing] was a great favourite – always laughing and joking. In the coach coming back after beating Swansea, spirits were high and the laughter loud at another of Mick's stories when our Honorary Treasurer, Air Commodore Warrington-Morris (Ret'd), commented how pleased he was to see that Mick appeared to be enjoying rugby union so much.

'Ee, I do that,' said Mick, 'have you ever sat in a rugby league coach having cost all the team a fifteen-quid-a-head bonus, after dropping the last scoring pass!?'

Dear old Warrington-Morris was never the same after that! Mind you, it didn't stop him crossing out an item on my travel expenses – 3/6d for a taxi, Kings Cross to the Waldorf and replacing it with 9d – bus!

* * *

I remember that wonderful moment when we played France B at Mont de Marsan when, after a kind of French 'Haka', our skipper, Lt Commander 'Squire' Wilkinson, led the Combined Services team in a superb rendering of 'Rule Britannia, Marmalade and Jam; three Chinese … etc., etc!'

* * *

Amazingly, only some three seasons later, out of the RAF blue came selection for the England v The Rest trial. I desperately turned over in my mind to whom I should turn for advice. How do you approach a trial? Who is the referee? What are they looking for and who has the final say in selection? I telephoned a great former England and Royal Navy lock and my Middlesex Captain, Johnnie Matthews, for advice. It was as succinct as was that of the Warrant Officer referee, and just as surprising.

'Peter,' he said, 'first you've got to make your mind up whether you are a press man or a selectors' man. They sit on opposite sides of the ground and you can't please all of them for 80 minutes! Personally, I'd go for the selectors but make sure you try to save a couple of good things for the press! Second, if you do something really good, tie up your laces with your back to the selectors, so they can read your number. If you do something terrible, run round all doubled up and dive in the nearest scrum!'

PHIL YATES

A snooker commentator for Sky TV and a BBC radio reporter.

They say that pride always comes before a fall and that was certainly the case when I was approached by a Scottish snooker fan at the Champion's reception of the Regal Masters in Motherwell during the mid-1990s.

'Well done, I've been listening to your commentary all week,' said the gentleman.

'Oh, so you've got Sky then,' I replied, chuffed to have been singled out for a wee bit of praise.

'No, I've been sitting in the front row,' he rasped.

It turned out that the commentary box had not been properly soundproofed. Consequently, my words of wisdom and indeed those of my co-commentator, Jim Wych, had been audible around the whole arena throughout the tournament.

NEIL YOUNG

Neil Young holds a cherished place in the heart of Manchester City supporters. Young was not only the club's leading scorer when they won the 1967–68 Division 1 championship ahead of Manchester United, but he also scored the winning goals in their 1969 FA Cup victory, and their Cup-Winners' Cup win one year later.

I was 17 years old, playing for Manchester City against Portsmouth FC away. I was eying up a blonde girl behind Portsmouth's goal.

We had a free kick outside the penalty area. I stood in the wall. As I turned round to have another look at the blonde girl, the free kick was taken and the ball hit me on the back of head and went into the top corner. I got back to Manchester and the *Pink Paper* wrote, 'Young scores winner with 18 yd power header.'

I signed for Preston, was given the cheque and told not to cash it.